Oracle PL/SQL
Programming Fundamentals
Second Edition

A Practical Tutorial by Examples

Table of Contents

New to the Second Edition

The second edition has three new chapters:
- Chapter 10: Records and Collection
- Chapter 11: Granting Privileges
- Chapter 12: PL/SQL in Java.

In Chapter 7: SQL in PL/SQL, the following topics were added:

- Transaction (controlling commit and rollback)
- Executing DDL statements

In Chapter 9: Subprograms, the following three topics were added:

- Stored Programs
- Package
- Trigger

Preface

Oracle PL/SQL Programming Fundamentals is for PL/SQL beginners. If you have no prior or limited skill of PL/SQL, and you want to learn the Oracle PL/SQL programming language the practical way, then this book is perfect for you.

Procedural Language extension of SQL

PL/SQL is the Oracle Procedural Language extension of SQL. PL/SQL is integrated within the Oracle database. When you install an Oracle database, PL/SQL is included in the installation. A PL/SQL program can have *both* SQL statements and procedural statements. In the program, the SQL statements are used to manipulate *sets* of data stored in a database, while the procedural statements are used to process *individual* piece of data and control the program flow, such as using the if-then-else and looping structures.

Using this book

The major topics covered in the book are listed in the Table of Contents.

When you finish reading the book and trying its examples, you would have equipped yourself with PL/SQL fundamental skills to start writing some PL/SQL programs for a real-world development project.

Prerequisite

You need SQL skills to successfully use this book. To learn or refresh your SQL skill, you can read my book: *Oracle SQL: A Beginner's Tutorial*.

Book Examples

To learn the most out of this book, try the book examples.

Set up your own Oracle database and SQL Developer tool to freely and safely try the examples. You can download free of charge both the database and the tool from the Oracle website.

Source codes of the book examples, including those for creating the example table (named *produce*) and inserting its rows, are listed in the *Appendix A: Source Codes*. If you don't want to type the examples, you can copy a source code from the appendix and paste it on your SQL Developer worksheet.

The examples were tested on Oracle Database 11g Express Edition release 2 and SQL Developer version 4.

Chapter 1: Setting Up

This first chapter is a guide to install and set up the Oracle Database 11g Expression Edition release 2 and SQL Developer version 4. Both are available at the Oracle website for download at no charge.

Installing Database Express Edition

Go to http://www.oracle.com/technetwork/indexes/downloads/index.html

Locate and download the Windows version of the Oracle Database Express Edition (XE). You will be requested to accept the license agreement. If you don't have one, create an account; it's free.

Unzip the downloaded file to a folder in your local drive, and then, double-click the setup.exe file.

You will see the Welcome window.

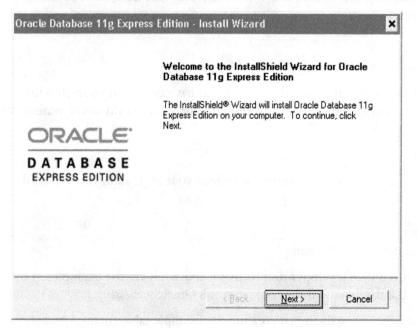

Click the Next> button, accept the agreement on the License Agreement window, and then click the Next> button again.

The next window is the "Choose Destination Location" window.

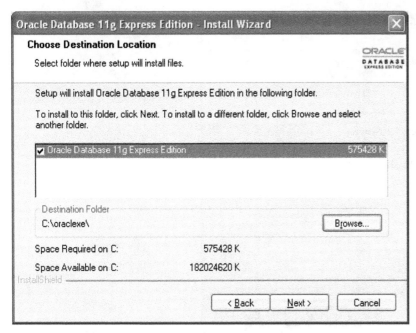

Accept the destination folder shown, or click the Browse button to choose a different folder for your installation, and then click the Next> button.

On the prompt for port numbers, accept the defaults, and then click the Next> button.

On the Passwords window, enter a password of your choice and confirm it, and then click the Next> button. The SYS and SYSTEM accounts created during this installation are for the database operation and administration, respectively. Note the password; you will use the SYSTEM account and its password for creating your own account, which you use for trying the examples.

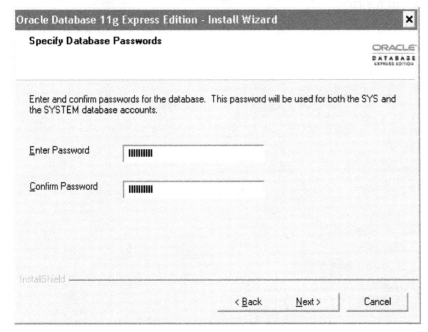

The Summary window will be displayed. Click Install.

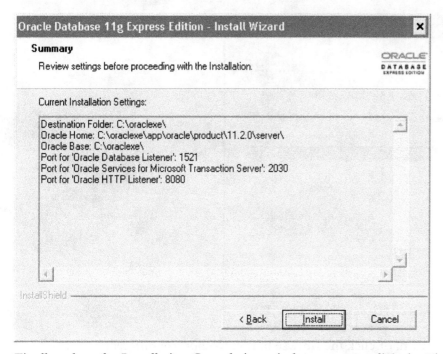

Finally, when the Installation Completion window appears, click the Finish button.

Your Oracle Database XE is now installed.

Installing SQL Developer

Go to http://www.oracle.com/technetwork/indexes/downloads/index.html

Locate and download the SQL Developer. You will be requested to accept the license agreement. If you don't have one, create an account; it's free.

Unzip the downloaded file to a folder of your preference. Note the folder name and its location; you will need to know them to start your SQL Developer.

When the unzipping is completed, look for the sqldeveloper.exe file.

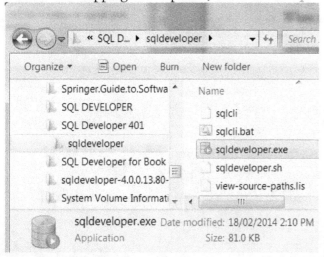

You start SQL Developer by opening (double-clicking) this file.

You might want to create a short-cut on your Desktop.

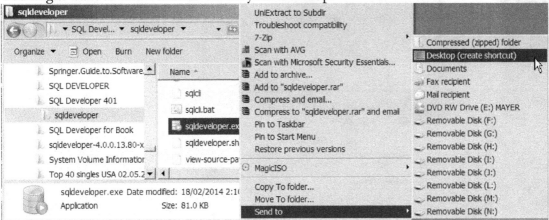

You can then start your SQL Developer by double-clicking the short-cut.

Your initial screen should look like the following. If you don't want to see the Start Page tab the next time you start SQL Developer, un-check the *Show on Startup* box at the bottom left side of the screen.

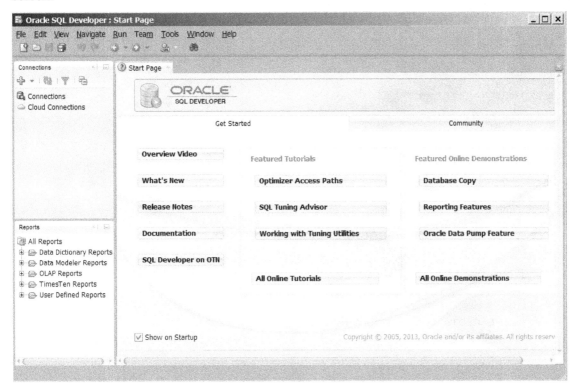

For now, close the Start Page tab by clicking its x.

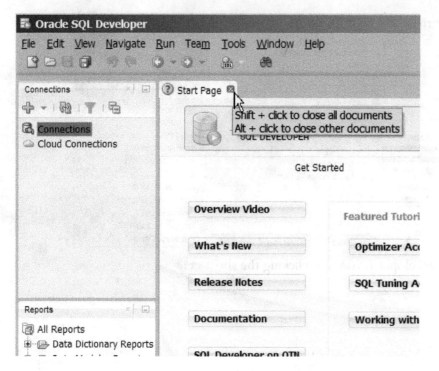

Creating Connection

To work with a database from SQL Developer, you need to have a connection.

A connection is specific to an account. As we will use the SYSTEM account to create your own account, you first have to create a connection for the SYSTEM account.

To create a connection, right-click the Connection folder.

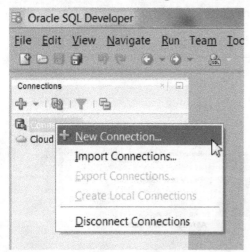

On the New/Select Database Connection window, enter a Connection Name and Username as shown. The Password is the password of SYSTEM account you entered during the Oracle database installation. Check the Save Password box.

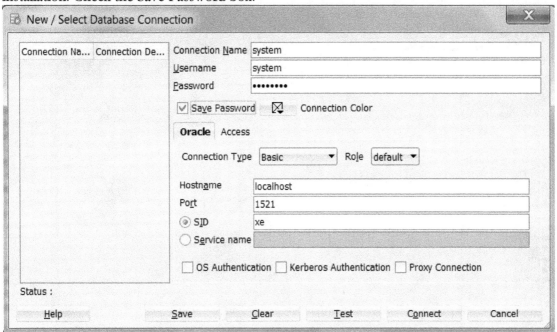

When you click the Connect button, the *system* connection you have just created should be available on the Connection Navigator.

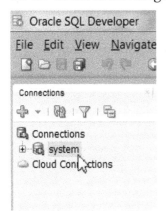

A Worksheet is opened for the system connection. The Worksheet is where you type in source codes.

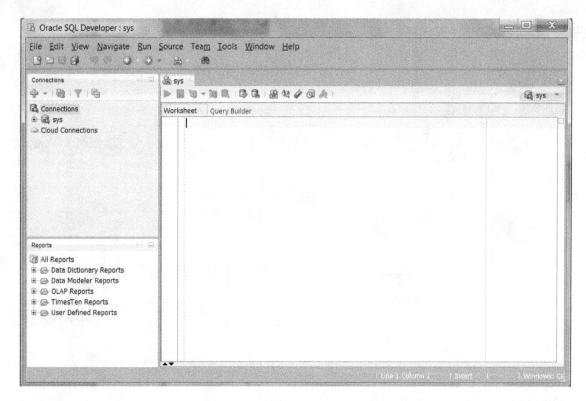

Creating Database Account

You will use your own database account (user) to try the book examples.

To create a new account, expand the system connection and locate the Other Users folder at the bottom of the folder tree.

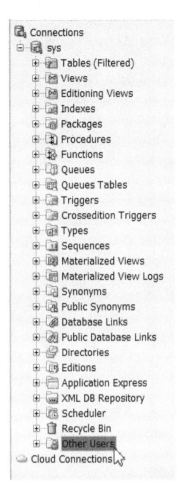

Right click and select Create User.

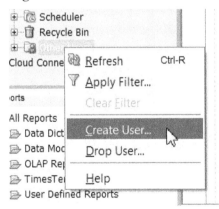

Enter a User Name of your choice, a password and its confirmation, and then click the Apply button. You should get a successful pop-up window; close it.

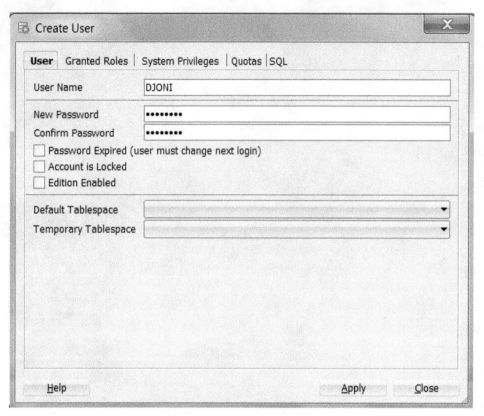

On the Granted Roles tab, click Grant All, Admin All and Default All buttons; then click the Apply button. Close the successful window and the Edit User as well.

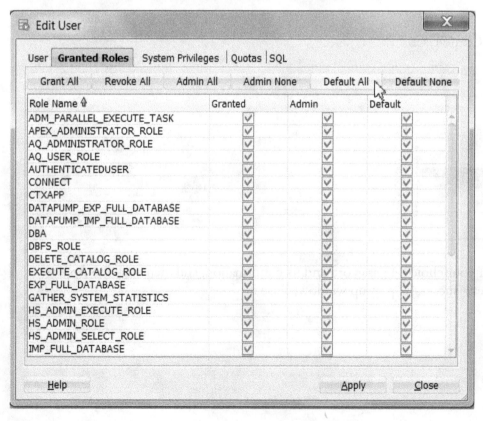

Creating Your Connection

Similar to when you created system connection earlier, now create a connection for your account.

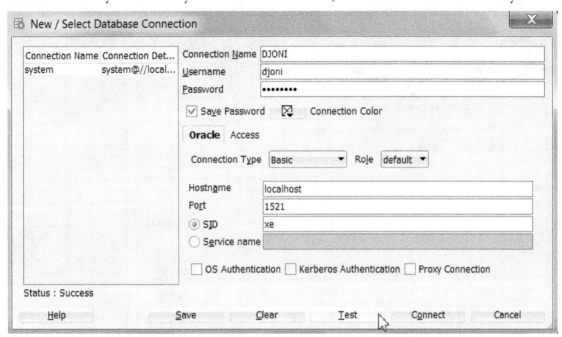

Click the Connect button. A worksheet for your connection is opened (which is *DJONI* in my case).

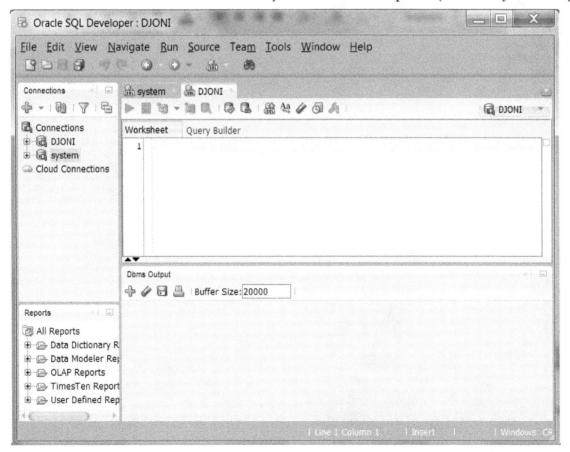

Showing Line Numbers

In describing the book examples I sometimes refer to the line numbers of the program; these are line numbers on the worksheet. To show line numbers, click Preferences from the Tools menu.

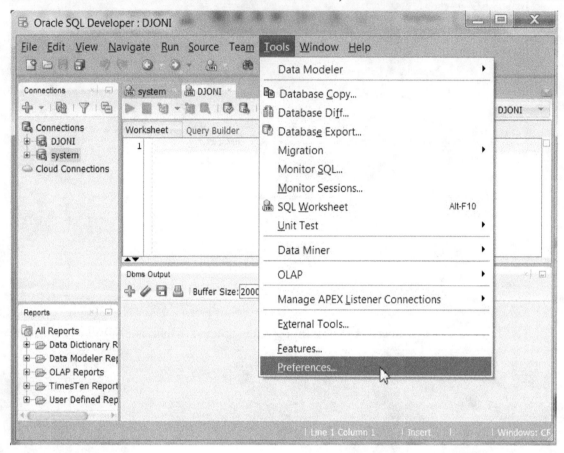

Select Line Gutter, then check the Show Line Numbers. Your Preferences should look like the following. Click the OK button.

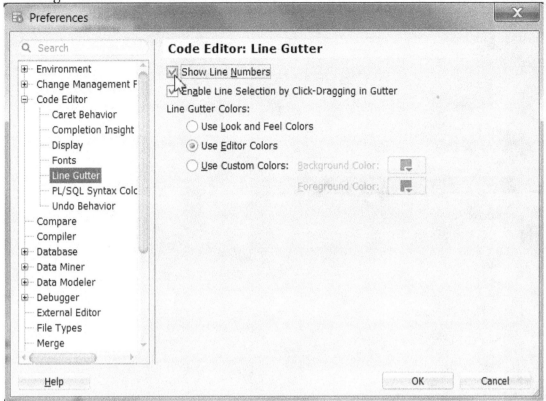

Deleting the *system* Connection

Delete the *system* connection, making sure you don't use this account mistakenly. Click Yes when you are prompted to confirm the deletion. Your SQL Developer is now set.

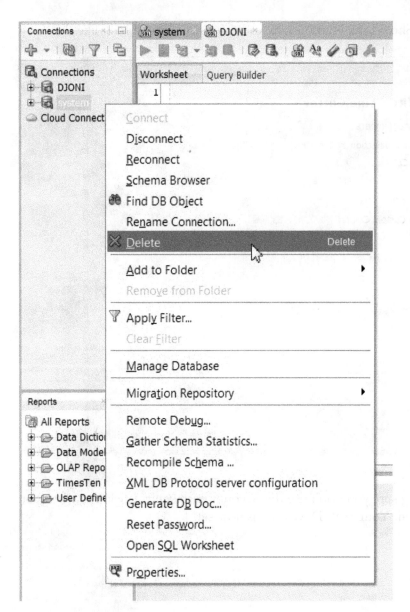

Close the *system* worksheet.

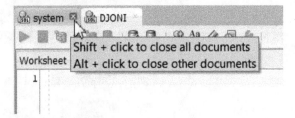

Chapter 2: Using SQL Developer

This chapter shows you how to use the SQL Developer features that you will use to try the book examples.

Entering SQL statement and PL/SQL source code

The worksheet is where you enter SQL statement and PL/SQL source code.

Start your SQL Developer if you have not done so. To open a worksheet for your connection, click the + (folder expansion) or double-click the connection name. Alternatively, right-click the connection and click Connect.

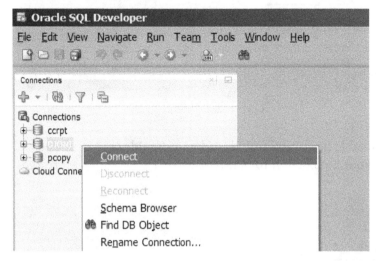

Note the name of the worksheet (tab label) is the name of your connection.

You can type source code on the worksheet.

Appendix A has the source code of all the book examples. Instead of typing, you can copy a source code and paste it on the worksheet.

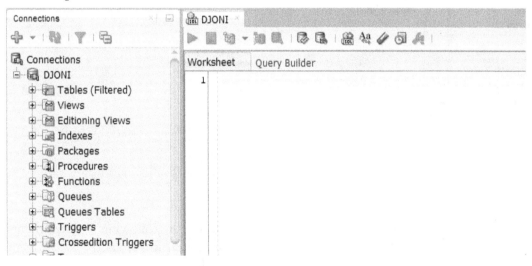

SQL Statement

Some of the book examples use a table named *produce*. Type in the SQL CREATE TABLE statement shown below to create the table (you might prefer to copy the *create_produce.sql* listing from Appendix A and paste it on your worksheet)

You run a SQL statement already in a worksheet by clicking the Run Statement button.

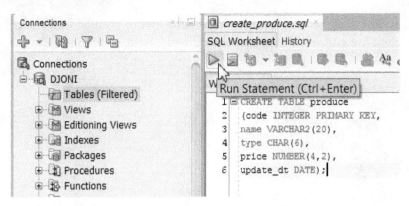

The Script Output pane confirms that the table has been created, and you should see the produce table in the Connection Navigator under your connection folder. If you don't see the newly created table, click Refresh.

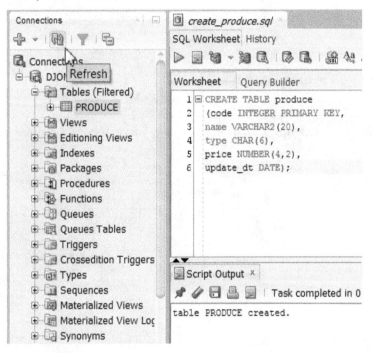

Inserting Rows

As an example of running multiple SQL statements in SQL Developer, the following five statements insert five rows into the produce table. Please type the statements, or copy it from *insert_produce.sql* in Appendix A. You will use these rows when you try the book examples.

Run all statements by clicking the Run Script button, or Ctrl+Enter (press and hold Ctrl button then click Enter button)

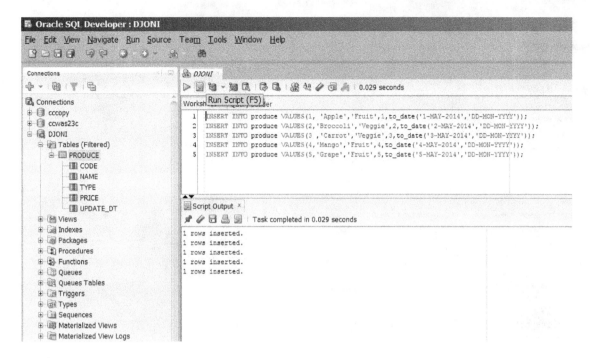

PL/SQL program

To learn how to run a PL/SQL program, type the following PL/SQL program, or copy it from *running_plsql.sql* in Appendix A.

You have not learned anything about PL/SQL programming yet, so don't worry what this program is all about.

To run the program, click the Run Script button or press F5.

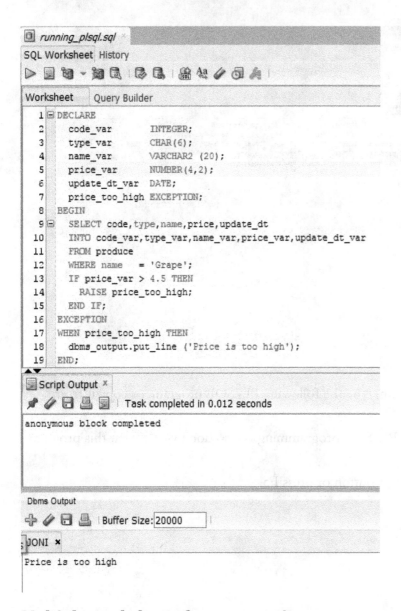

```
running_plsql.sql
SQL Worksheet  History

Worksheet    Query Builder
 1 □ DECLARE
 2     code_var        INTEGER;
 3     type_var        CHAR(6);
 4     name_var        VARCHAR2 (20);
 5     price_var       NUMBER(4,2);
 6     update_dt_var   DATE;
 7     price_too_high  EXCEPTION;
 8   BEGIN
 9 □   SELECT code,type,name,price,update_dt
10     INTO code_var,type_var,name_var,price_var,update_dt_var
11     FROM produce
12     WHERE name   = 'Grape';
13     IF price_var > 4.5 THEN
14       RAISE price_too_high;
15     END IF;
16   EXCEPTION
17   WHEN price_too_high THEN
18     dbms_output.put_line ('Price is too high');
19   END;
```

Script Output ×

Task completed in 0.012 seconds

anonymous block completed

Dbms Output

Buffer Size: 20000

JONI ×

Price is too high

Multiple worksheets for a connection

Sometimes you need to have two or more programs on different worksheets. You can open more than one worksheet for a connection by right-clicking the connection and select Open SQL Worksheet.

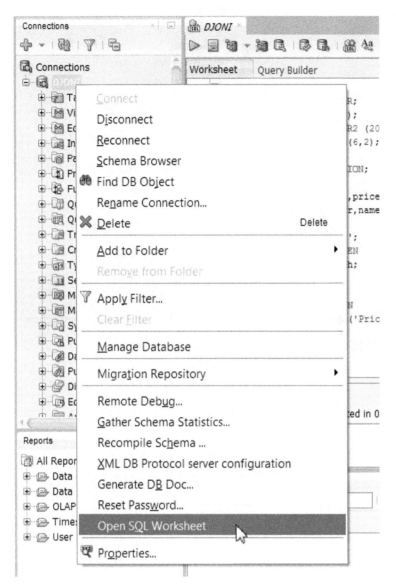

The names of the next tabs for a connection have sequential numbers added.

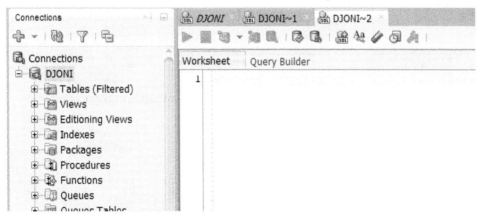

Storing the source code

You can store a source code into a text file for later re-opening by selecting Save from the File menu.

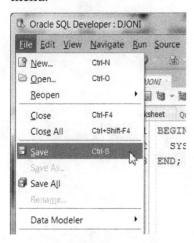

Select the location where you want to store the source code and give the file a name, and then click Save.

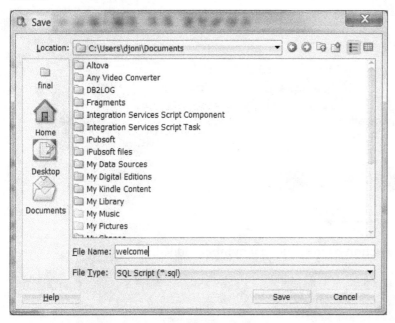

Opening a source code

You can open a source code by selecting Open or Reopen from the File menu and then select the file that contains the source code.

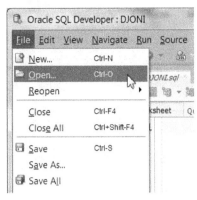

The source code will be opened on a new worksheet. The tab of the worksheet has the name of the file. The following is the worksheet opened for the source code stored as file named running_plsql.sql.

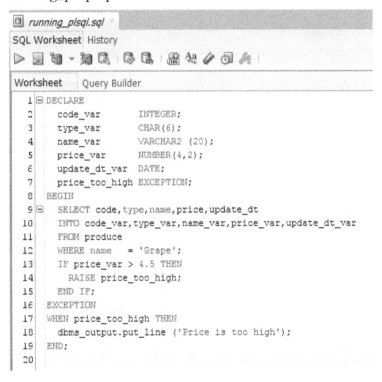

Storing the listings in Appendix A into files

As an alternative to copy and paste, you can store each of the listing into a file and then you can open the file. Note that you must store each program source code into a file.

Running SQL or PL/SQL from a file

You can execute a file that contains SQL statement or PL/SQL program without opening it on the worksheet as shown here.

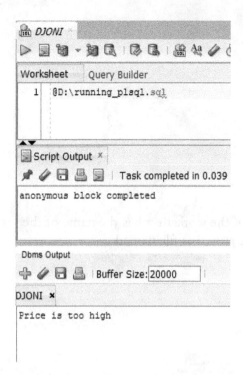

Clearing a Worksheet

To clear a Worksheet, click its Clear button.

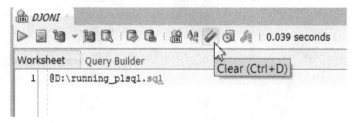

Displaying Output

Most of the book examples use the Oracle-supplied dbms_output.put_line procedure to display some outputs. For the book readers learning PL/SQL, the displayed output gives an instant feedback of what happens in the running program. Real-life programs might not need to display any output.

The dbms_output.put_line procedure has the following syntax.

```
dbms_output.put_line (parameter);
```

The value of the parameter must evaluate to a string literal (value).

When the procedure is executed in SQL Developer, the string literal is displayed on the Dbms Output.

To see the output, before you run the example, make sure you already have a Dbms Output pane opened for the connection you use to run the program. If your Dbms Output is not ready, set it up as follows:

Assume you want to run the program as shown here.

Click the View menu.

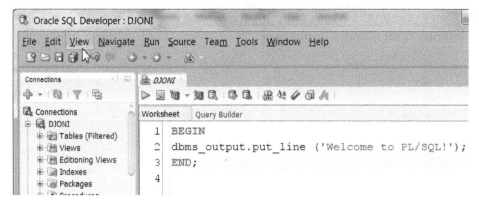

Next, select Dbms Output.

The Dbms Output pane is now opened.

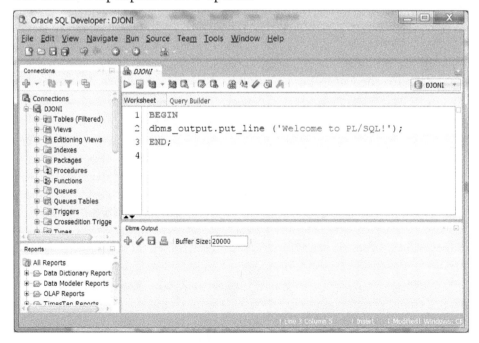

To display an output, you need to set up the Dbms Output pane for the connection you use to run the program. Click the + button on the Dbms Output pane.

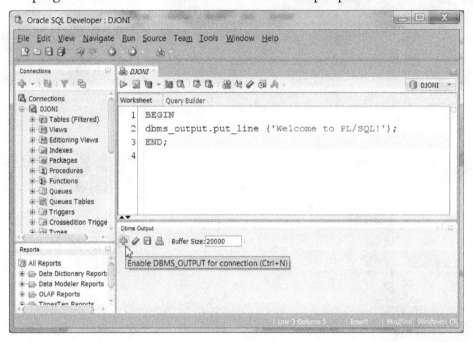

On the pop-up window, select the connection, and then click OK. As an example I select DJONI connection as this is the connection I want to use for running my PL/SQL program.

The Dbms Output now has the tab for the DJONI connection.

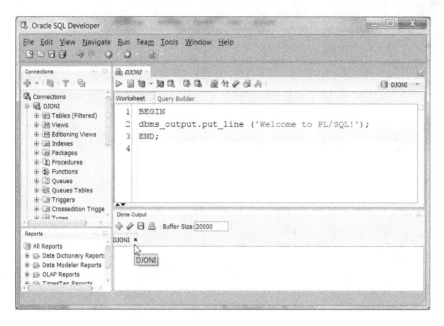

Now, run the program by clicking the Run Statement button. The Dbms Output pane displays the "Welcome to PL/SQL!" greeting. The message on the Script Output pane shows the result of running the program; in this case it indicates that the program is completed successfully. It would show an error message if the program is having a problem.

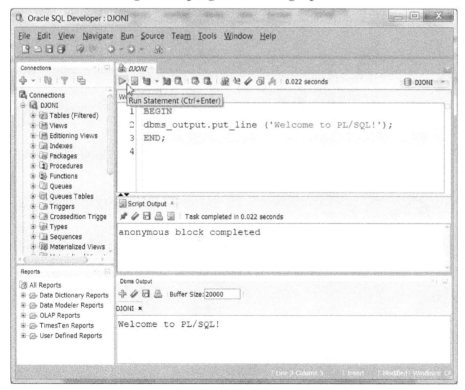

Clearing Dbms Output

To see a display output from a program, you might want to erase the output from a previous program. To clear a Dbms Output, click its Clear button.

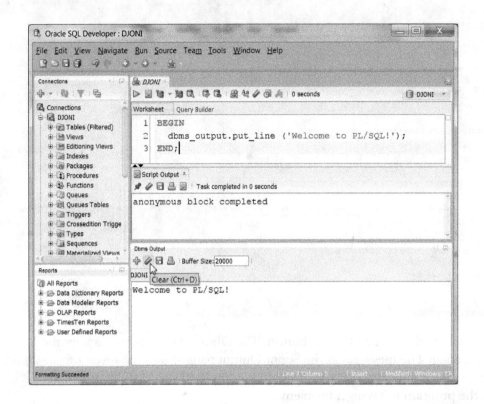

Chapter 3: Block

PL/SQL is a block-structured programming language. A PL/SQL program consists of one or more blocks. (You will later learn about multiple-blocks in the **Nesting Block** section of this chapter)

A block has three parts: Declaration, Executable and Exception-handling. A block has the following structure.

```
DECLARE
  Declaration
BEGIN
  Executable
EXCEPTION
  Exception-handling
END;
```

The three parts of a block are separated by the DECLARE, BEGIN, EXCEPTION, and END PL/SQL reserved words. You should not use any reserved word for any other than its designated purpose.

Declaration Part

Variables used to hold **program** data are declared in the Declaration part. (Data stored in a database must be read into program variables to be processed in the program)

All declaration statements must be located between the DECLARATION and BEGIN reserved words.

The syntax of a variable declaration is.

```
variable data_type;
```

On the Example 3-1.sql worksheet, shown on the right side of the following screenshot, is a program with one block and five variables. Lines 2 – 6 are the declaration statements of these variables. Their datatypes are INTEGER, CHAR (to hold a fixed-length string of characters), VARCHAR2 (to hold a variable-length string of characters), NUMBER, and DATE.

These five variables are used on line 9 by the SELECT INTO query statement. The variables hold the values of the five columns returned by the query.

The SELECT statement on line 8 – 11 queries the produce table. The table has the five rows that you entered in Chapter 2, shown on the left side of the screenshot.

When you run the program, it will complete successfully as indicated by the message on the Script Output pane.

The dbms_output.put_line displays the data held by the five variables as shown on the Dbms Output pane at the bottom of the screenshot.

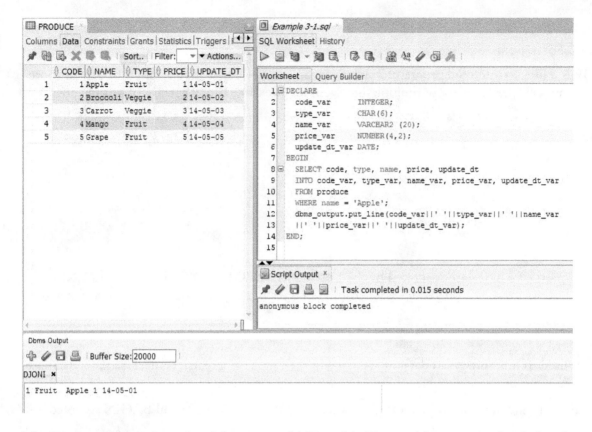

The Declaration part is optional, but any variable used in Executable part must be declared; otherwise, the program will fail.

In Example 3-2, code_var used in the INTO clause (line 8) is not declared. When you run the program, the PL/SQL compiler complains that code_var was not declared, the program fails and gets aborted.

Declaring Other Program Objects

In addition to variable, you can also declare other program objects, such as Constant and Exception. You will learn these in Chapter 4.

Executable Part

A block must have an Executable part, which in turn must have at least one statement. The Declaration and Exception-handling parts are optional.

Example 3-3 has the Executable part only with one statement only. It does not require any declaration as the Executable does not require any variable. The program successfully displays the string literal *Welcome to PL/SQL!*

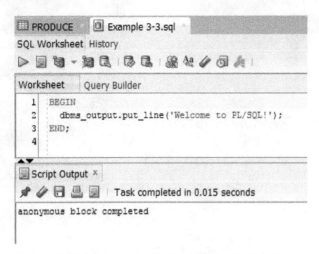

You might have noticed that, while declaration statements **define** variables, executable statements **perform** something on variables.

You will learn more about the Executable part in Chapter 5.

Exception-handling Part

The Exception-handling part allows you to specify the actions to execute when the program encounters a runtime error.

Line 4 of Example 3-4 tries to assign a literal that is six characters long to the x variable that is declared with maximum length of five characters. When you run Example 3.4, the program will abort.

You can avoid the failure by adding an exception handler. The syntax of the exception statement is

```
WHEN exception THEN statement;
```

Example 3-5 has an Exception-handling part on line 5 – 7. The OTHERS exception handles all other errors not handled by any other exception-handler. This example happens to have only the OTHERS, so this handler will take care of any runtime error.

When you run the program, it will get completed successfully, it does not abort. The Dbms Output has the error message you would like to be shown when a runtime exception occurs.

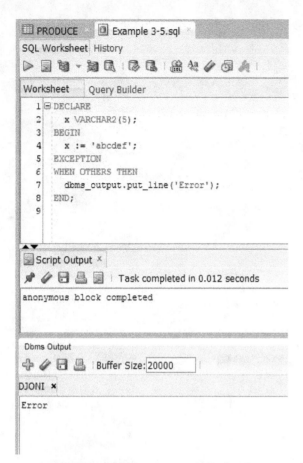

You will learn more about the Exception-handling part in Chapter 6.

Block Nesting

You can write a program with multiple blocks by nesting a block under another block.

In the Executable part of Example 3-6 we have a total of four blocks with three levels of nesting. Line 1 – 12 is the outermost (parent) block; it is the first level of nesting. The parent block has two (children) nested blocks; they are the second level of nesting. Line 3 – 5 is the first child and line 6 – 11 is the second child. Line 8 – 10 is a (grandchild) nested block within the second child; the grandchild is at the third level of nesting.

```
  1 □ BEGIN
  2    dbms_output.put_line('Parent block');
  3    BEGIN
  4      dbms_output.put_line('  First child nested block');
  5    END;
  6 □  BEGIN
  7        dbms_output.put_line('  Second child nested block');
  8      BEGIN
  9        dbms_output.put_line('    Grandchild nested block of 1st child');
 10      END;
 11    END;
 12  END;
 13
```

Script Output ×

Task completed in 0.007 seconds

anonymous block completed

Dbms Output

Buffer Size: 20000

DJONI ×

```
Parent block
  First child nested block
  Second child nested block
    Grandchild nested block of 1st child
```

Block Label

You label a block at its beginning with <<*label*>> syntax and at the end with END *label*. The label at the end is optional, but having it there clarifies the block's scope: all parts and their statements of the block are those between its beginning label and end label pair.

All four blocks in Example 3.7 are labeled. In this example, each of the blocks has only one executable statement; they could well have as many statements and as complex as the program needs to.

A label is not an executable statement; Example 3-7 produces the same result as Example 3.6.

```
  1   << parent >>
  2   BEGIN
  3     dbms_output.put_line('Parent block');
  4     << first_child >>
  5     BEGIN
  6       dbms_output.put_line('  First child nested block');
  7     END first_child;
  8     << second_child >>
  9     BEGIN
 10         dbms_output.put_line('  Second child nested block');
 11       << grandchild >>
 12       BEGIN
 13         dbms_output.put_line('    Grandchild nested block of 1st child');
 14       END grandchild;
 15     END second_child;
 16   END parent;
 17
```

Script Output ×

Task completed in 0.006 seconds

anonymous block completed

Dbms Output

Buffer Size: 20000

DJONI ×

```
Parent block
  First child nested block
  Second child nested block
    Grandchild nested block of 1st child
```

Nesting in Exception-handling part

All previous nesting's are in the Executable part. You can also nest a block in the Exception-handling part as demonstrated in Example 3-8. The parent block starting on line 12 has a child block that starts on line 15.

The parent block has an Exception-handling part; the child block, if it needs to, could have as well.

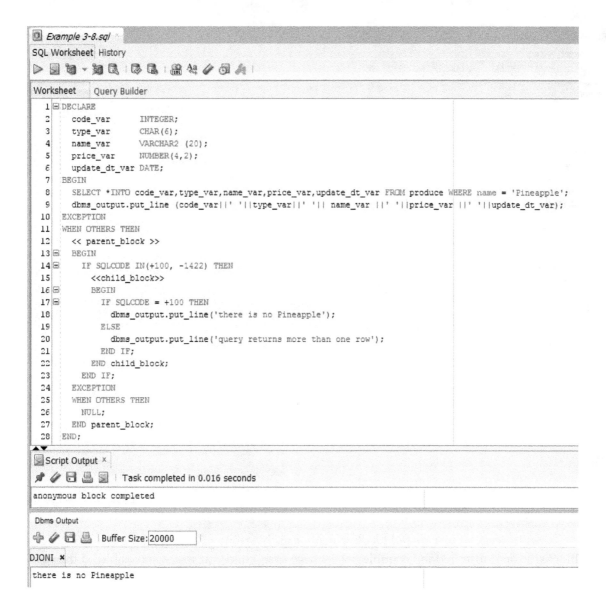

```
Example 3-8.sql

SQL Worksheet   History

Worksheet   Query Builder

1  DECLARE
2     code_var       INTEGER;
3     type_var       CHAR(6);
4     name_var       VARCHAR2 (20);
5     price_var      NUMBER(4,2);
6     update_dt_var DATE;
7  BEGIN
8     SELECT *INTO code_var,type_var,name_var,price_var,update_dt_var FROM produce WHERE name = 'Pineapple';
9     dbms_output.put_line (code_var||' '||type_var||' '|| name_var ||' '||price_var ||' '||update_dt_var);
10 EXCEPTION
11 WHEN OTHERS THEN
12    << parent_block >>
13    BEGIN
14      IF SQLCODE IN(+100, -1422) THEN
15        <<child_block>>
16        BEGIN
17          IF SQLCODE = +100 THEN
18            dbms_output.put_line('there is no Pineapple');
19          ELSE
20            dbms_output.put_line('query returns more than one row');
21          END IF;
22        END child_block;
23      END IF;
24    EXCEPTION
25    WHEN OTHERS THEN
26      NULL;
27    END parent_block;
28 END;
```

Script Output ×

📌 ✏ 💾 🖨 🖥   Task completed in 0.016 seconds

anonymous block completed

Dbms Output

➕ ✏ 💾 🖨   Buffer Size: 20000

DJONI ×

there is no Pineapple

Variable Visibility

A variable is visible (can be used) in all its nested blocks. In Example 3-9, the parent_var declared on line 3 is visible in its child's block (line 11).

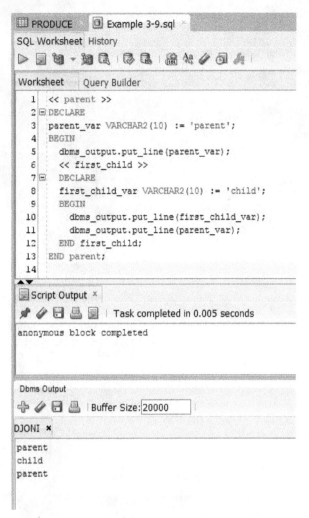

However, a variable declared in a nested block is neither visible to its parent block nor to other children blocks, as demonstrated in Example 3-10 where first_child_var is not accessible by the statement on line 6 and the statement of line 16.

Same-Name Variables

If you have a variable with the same name in two blocks, you can refer to which one of the variable by using their labels with a dot notation.

The parent.same_name_var in Example 3-11 is example. The statement on line 11 displays the value of the parent's same_name_var.

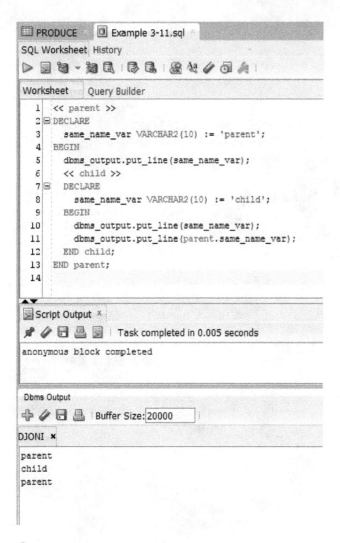

```
     << parent >>
   DECLARE
     same_name_var VARCHAR2(10) := 'parent';
   BEGIN
     dbms_output.put_line(same_name_var);
     << child >>
   DECLARE
     same_name_var VARCHAR2(10) := 'child';
   BEGIN
     dbms_output.put_line(same_name_var);
     dbms_output.put_line(parent.same_name_var);
   END child;
   END parent;
```

Script Output ✕

Task completed in 0.005 seconds

anonymous block completed

Dbms Output

Buffer Size: 20000

DJONI ✕

```
parent
child
parent
```

Comment

Any text in a source code following a double dash -- is a single-line comment. When a /* mark is encountered, all lines that follow until a closing */ mark is a multi-line comment.

Example 3-12 has two single-line comments on the top, two single-comments on line 4 and 5, which do not start at the beginning of the lines, and one multiline comment, which starts on line 7 and end on line 8.

Comments are ignored, not compiled, hence not part of a program. They serve as inline documentation in the source code.

Example 3-12.sql

SQL Worksheet History

Worksheet   Query Builder

```
 1    -- Example 3-12: Comments
 2    -- An example of declaring a constant and a variable
 3  DECLARE
 4      fruit_con   CONSTANT VARCHAR2(20) := 'Fruit';  -- constant example
 5      veggie_var VARCHAR2(20)            := 'Veggie'; -- variable example
 6    BEGIN
 7      /* the following SQL adds a produce
 8      into the produce table */
 9      INSERT
10      INTO produce VALUES
11        (99,'Tangerine',fruit_con, 9 , '1-JAN-2014' );
12    END;
13
```

Chapter 4: Variable Declaration

Variable is introduced in Chapter 2. A variable is used to hold (store) **program** data. Here is the syntax again:

```
variable datatype;
```

A variable name must start with a letter; the rest can be letters, digits, or any of the following three symbols: _ (underscore), # (number sign), and $ (dollar sign). The maximum length of a name is 30 characters. Additionally, PL/SQL is not case sensitive.

The following four variable names, for example, are not valid.

```
9code_var -- start with numeric
Name_var% -- has a % character
price var -- has a blank
Date_the_price_of_this_produce_was_changed_var -- longer than 30 characters
```

Datatype

When you declare a variable, you must specify its datatype.

We have used the following five datatypes in Chapter 3:

- INTEGER to store numeric integer type of data
- CHAR to store fixed length string of characters
- VARCHAR2(m) to store a variable length string of characters to a maximum of m characters
- NUMBER(p, s) to store numeric data with precision of p digits and scale of s digits
- DATE to store date

Other Datatypes

In addition to these five datatypes, PL/SQL supports other datatypes such as FLOAT (floating point number) and CLOB (Character Large Object Binary). Please consult the Oracle manuals available online on the Oracle website about the other datatypes not covered in this book.

In Chapter 7 you will learn PL/SQL special datatypes: ROWTYPE and TYPE.

Storing Data in Variables

You can store columns from SELECT INTO statement into variables or by assigning a value locally within the program using the assignment operator :=

SELECT INTO statement

A SELECT INTO statement reads a row of data from a table and stores the data into variables. The SELECT INTO statement on line 8 - 11 of Example 4-1 is an example. Line 12 – 13 confirms that the Apple data from the table are stored in the five variables by displaying them.

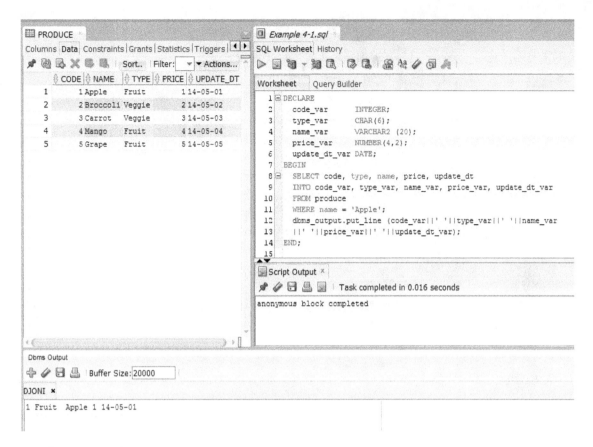

Assignment Operator

The use of the assignment operator **:=** to store data into a variable is demonstrated on line 12 of Example 4-2, where a literal 'New ' is concatenated with the data being stored in the name_var (| | is the concatenated operator)

The new_name_var variable is then used to update the 'Apple' into "New Apple".

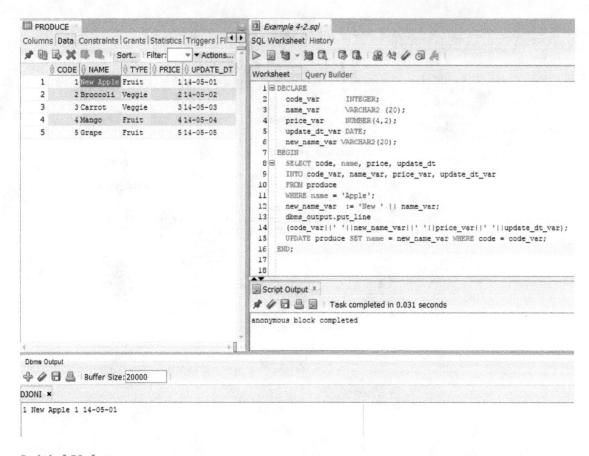

Initial Value

An initial value can be assigned to a variable; its syntax is:

```
variable data_type := 'initial_value';
```

If an initialized variable is then used without changing its initial value, the initial value is applied as-is; in other words, the initial value is the default value of the variable. Hence, an alternative syntax for the same purpose, with the DEFAULT reserved word instead of the := operator, is:

```
variable data_type DEFAULT 'initial_value';
```

If a variable is not initialized to NULL (NULL means no value)

On line 8 of Example 4-3, the new_var variable is initialized to a 'New ' value. Line 14 concatenates this 'New ' with the original name of the produce read by the query. Line 15 displays the result of the concatenation stored in the new_name_var.

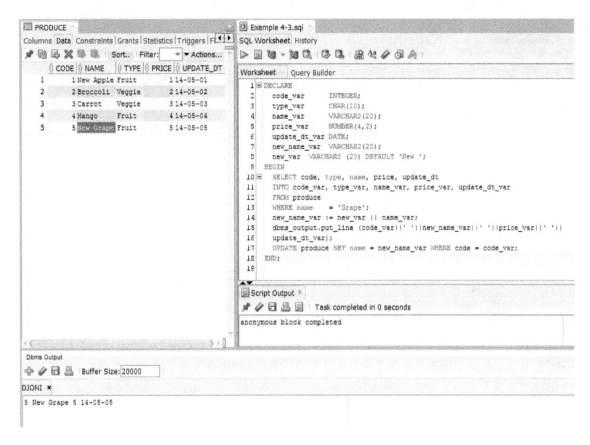

NOT NULL

You can assure a variable to always hold a value by adding a clause NOT NULL; such a variable must be initialized. Its syntax is hence as follows.

```
variable data_type NOT NULL := 'initial_value';
```

Please insert a new row with code 99 as shown here. Don't enter any data on the other columns.

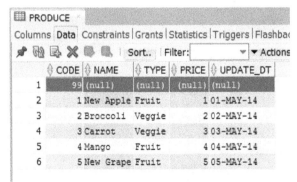

In Example 4-4 none of the variables has the NOT NULL clause; the last four get populated with NULL's by the SELECT INTO statement on line 8 – 11 without any error.

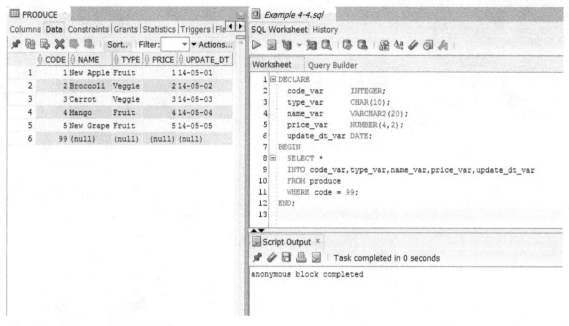

Line 3 of Example 4-5 declares type_var as NOT NULL. The program fails because the SELECT INTO tries to store NULL from the 99 produce into the type_var.

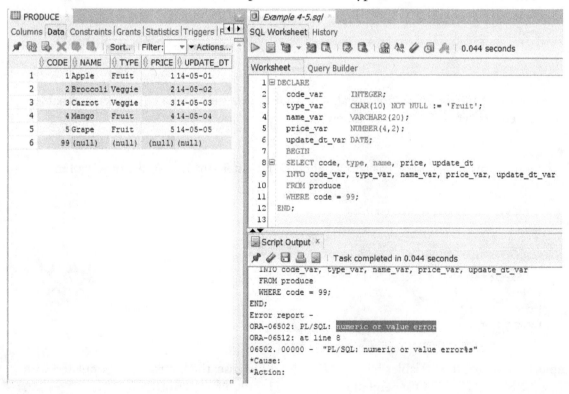

Constant

A constant is a 'variable' that holds a value for life; its declaration syntax is:

```
constant_name CONSTANT data_type := 'constant_value';
```

You can then use the constant_name in the Executable part to represent the constant_value.

Example 4-6 declares two constants. The fruit_con and veggie_con are then used by the INSERT statements to populate the type of Tangerine and Lettuce.

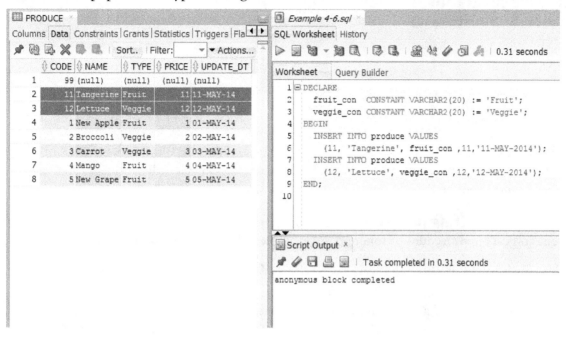

You can't change the value of a constant. Example 4-7 fails trying to change the value of the fruit_con.

Chapter 5: Executable Statement

Here is the block structure again.

```
DECLARE
    Declaration
BEGIN
    Executable
EXCEPTION
    Exception handler
END;
```

All executable statements must be located after the BEGIN and EXCEPTION reserved words. As the Exception-handler part is optional, if a program does not have it, then all executable statements must be located between the BEGIN and END reserved words.

Assignment and Calling procedure and function

Assignment and calling procedure or function are examples of executable statements.

An assignment statement uses the statement operator := to store data into a variable.

In Example 5-1, line 8, 9, 10 and 11, are assignment statements. Line 8 and 9 store a numeric literal 20 into code_var variable and a string literal 'Kale' into name_var variable, respectively. Line 10 stores the result of the sum of price_var variable (the 2.5 initial value currently stored in the variable) and a numeric literal 1.0, into price_var.

Line 11 stores the date returned from the Oracle-supplied CURRENT_DATE function; this function returns the current date.

Line 12 calls the dbms_output.put_line to display its parameter, the four variables.

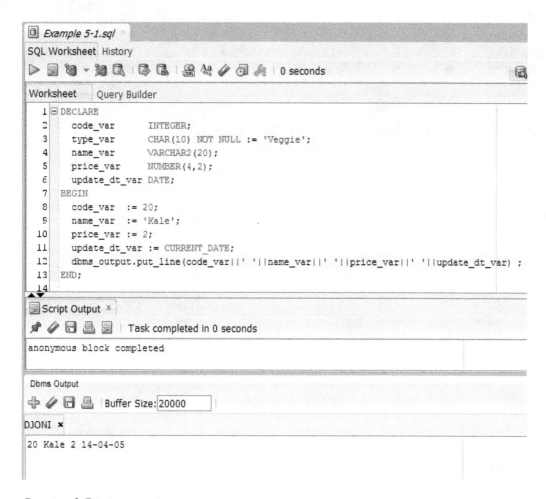

Control Statements

To control program flows, you use conditional and loop statements.

IF THEN

The syntax of the IF THEN statement is.

```
IF condition THEN
   statements;
END IF;
```

Only if the condition is true the statements will be executed.

Example 5-2 has an IF THEN statement on line 6 –10. ROUND on line 8 is an Oracle-supplied function, it returns its argument rounded to its integer value. In the example, the argument is num.

When you run the program, you will be prompted to enter a number that will be stored in the num variable. (To prompt an input value use & as a prefix to the prompt label; in Example 5.2 it is &num_input, hence the prompt window shows the num_input label. If you want to prompt for a string/alphanumeric value, surround the prompt label with single quotes, for example, '&var_input')

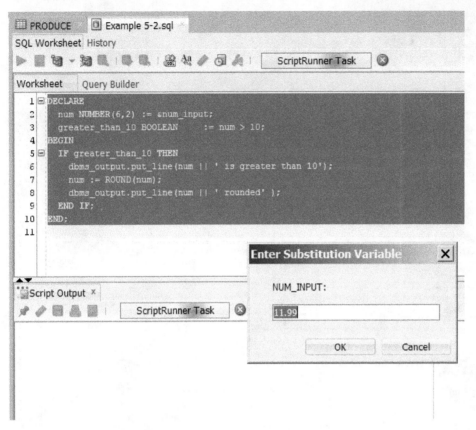

If on the prompt you enter a number greater than 10 (such as 11.99), the three statements on lines 6 – 8 will be executed and displayed; if smaller than 10, these statements will not be executed.

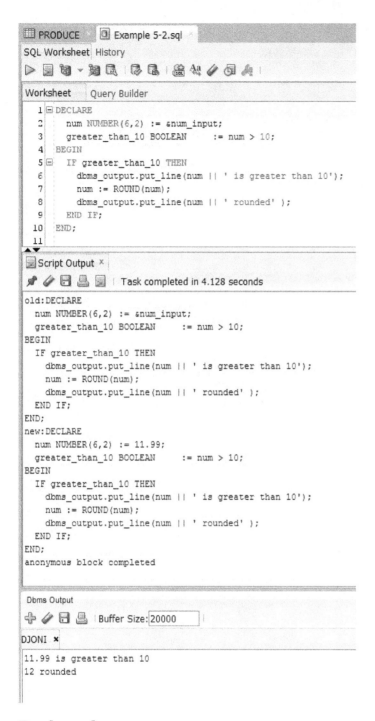

Boolean datatype

A Boolean variable can be true or false.

While in Example 5-2, the IF condition is hardcoded, Example 5-3 uses a Boolean variable as the condition. The greater_than_10 variable is declared on line 3 as true if *num* is greater than 10. It is then used as a condition on line 5.

When you run Example 5.3 and enter the same value as you did on Example 5-2, you will get the same result.

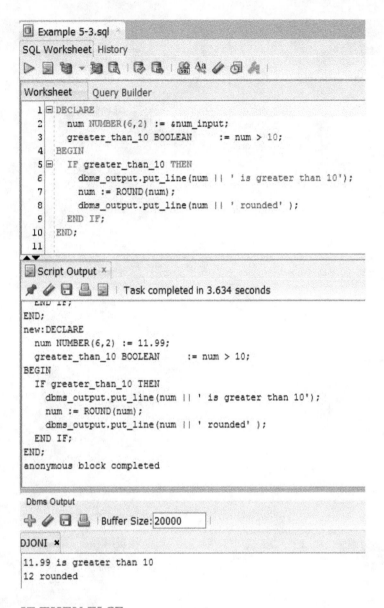

IF THEN ELSE

The syntax of the IF THEN ELSE statement is.

```
IF condition THEN
   if_statements;
ELSE
   else_statements;
END IF;
```

An IF THEN ELSE executes its if_statements if its condition is true. If the condition is false, the else_statements are executed.

Example 5-4 has an IF THEN ELSE statements on lines 5 – 9. If you enter a value greater than 10, line 6 will be executed; if equal or smaller than 10, line 8 will be executed.

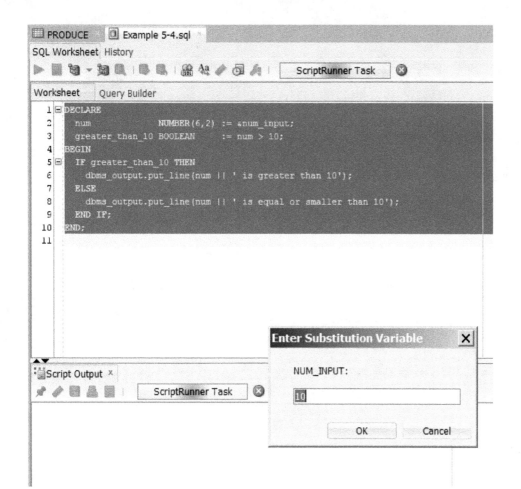

```
PRODUCE          Example 5-4.sql
SQL Worksheet  History

                              ScriptRunner Task      ⊗

Worksheet    Query Builder

 1 ⊟ DECLARE
 2      num              NUMBER(6,2)  := &num_input;
 3      greater_than_10 BOOLEAN       := num > 10;
 4   BEGIN
 5 ⊟   IF greater_than_10 THEN
 6        dbms_output.put_line(num || ' is greater than 10');
 7      ELSE
 8        dbms_output.put_line(num || ' is equal or smaller than 10');
 9      END IF;
10   END;
11
```

Script Output ×

ScriptRunner Task   ⊗

Enter Substitution Variable   ✕

NUM_INPUT:

10

OK   Cancel

```
PRODUCE    Example 5-4.sql
SQL Worksheet  History
                                              65.79100037 seconds
Worksheet    Query Builder
  1  DECLARE
  2      num               NUMBER(6,2) := &num_input;
  3      greater_than_10 BOOLEAN      := num > 10;
  4  BEGIN
  5      IF greater_than_10 THEN
  6        dbms_output.put_line(num || ' is greater than 10');
  7      ELSE
  8        dbms_output.put_line(num || ' is equal or smaller than 10');
  9      END IF;
 10  END;
 11
```

```
Script Output ×
               Task completed in 65.791 seconds
old:DECLARE
  num               NUMBER(6,2) := &num_input;
  greater_than_10 BOOLEAN      := num > 10;
BEGIN
  IF greater_than_10 THEN
    dbms_output.put_line(num || ' is greater than 10');
  ELSE
    dbms_output.put_line(num || ' is equal or smaller than 10');
  END IF;
END;
new:DECLARE
  num               NUMBER(6,2) := 10;
  greater_than_10 BOOLEAN      := num > 10;
BEGIN
  IF greater_than_10 THEN
    dbms_output.put_line(num || ' is greater than 10');
  ELSE
    dbms_output.put_line(num || ' is equal or smaller than 10');
  END IF;
END;
anonymous block completed
```

```
Dbms Output
              Buffer Size: 20000
DJONI ×
10 is equal or smaller than 10
```

IF THEN ELSIF

If you need multiple ELSE's, then use an IF THEN ELSIF statement. Its syntax is as follows.

```
IF condition_1 THEN
  statements_1;
ELSIF condition_2 THEN
  statements_2;
ELSIF ...
[ ELSE
  else_statements ]
END IF;
```

The IF THEN ELSIF statement executes only the first statement for which its condition is true; the remaining conditions are not evaluated. If no condition is true, then the else_statements are executed, if they exist; otherwise, the IF THEN ELSIF statement does nothing.

The ELSE is optional.

Example 5-5 has an IF THEN ELSIF statement on lines 5 – 11. Its output depends on the input you enter on the prompt. If you enter a value greater than 10 then line 6 is executed; if equal to 10 than line 8 is executed; if less than 10, line 10 will be executed.

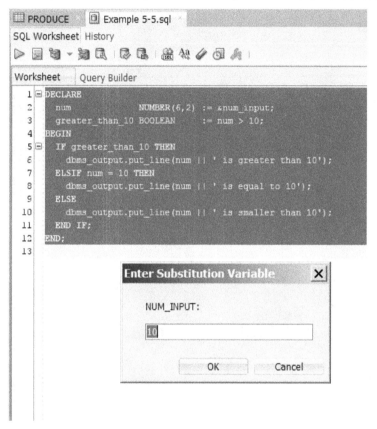

```
  1  DECLARE
  2    num              NUMBER(6,2) := &num_input;
  3    greater_than_10 BOOLEAN      := num > 10;
  4  BEGIN
  5    IF greater_than_10 THEN
  6      dbms_output.put_line(num || ' is greater than 10');
  7    ELSIF num = 10 THEN
  8      dbms_output.put_line(num || ' is equal to 10');
  9    ELSE
 10      dbms_output.put_line(num || ' is smaller than 10');
 11    END IF;
 12  END;
 13
```

Script Output ×

Task completed in 3.11 seconds

```
old:DECLARE
  num              NUMBER(6,2) := &num_input;
  greater_than_10 BOOLEAN      := num > 10;
BEGIN
  IF greater_than_10 THEN
    dbms_output.put_line(num || ' is greater than 10');
  ELSIF num = 10 THEN
    dbms_output.put_line(num || ' is equal to 10');
  ELSE
    dbms_output.put_line(num || ' is smaller than 10');
  END IF;
END;
new:DECLARE
  num              NUMBER(6,2) := 10;
  greater_than_10 BOOLEAN      := num > 10;
BEGIN
  IF greater_than_10 THEN
    dbms_output.put_line(num || ' is greater than 10');
  ELSIF num = 10 THEN
    dbms_output.put_line(num || ' is equal to 10');
  ELSE
    dbms_output.put_line(num || ' is smaller than 10');
  END IF;
```

Dbms Output

Buffer Size: 20000

DJONI ×

```
10 is equal to 10
```

Simple CASE

The syntax of the Simple CASE statement is.

```
CASE selector
WHEN selector_value_1 THEN statements_1
WHEN selector_value_2 THEN statements_2
WHEN ...
[ ELSE else_statements ]
END CASE;
```

The selector is a variable. Each selector_value can be either a literal or a variable.

The simple CASE statement runs the first statement for which its selector_value equals the selector. Remaining conditions are not evaluated. If no selector_value equals selector, the CASE statement runs else_statements if they exist; or raises the predefined exception CASE_NOT_FOUND otherwise.

The ELSE is optional.

The selector in the Simple CASE statement (lines 4 – 15) of Example 5-6 is the variable clue. The statement has four WHEN's, each with a literal as its selector value; the first WHEN's selector value, for example, is literal 'O'. If the clue value you enter on the prompt is not any one of the selector value's, the ELSE statement, line 14, will be executed.

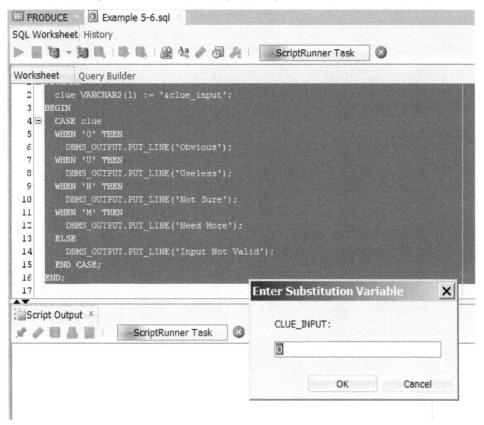

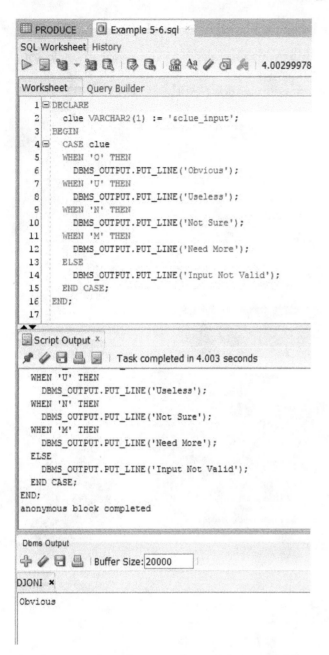

A selector and a selector_value can be a variable or an expression; and you can have more than one selector_value variable. In Example 5-7, the selector is sel_in; and this CASE has two selector_value variables: the first selector is sel_in_1 variable; the second, sel_in_2.

When you run the program, you will be prompted three times for the values of sel, sel_value_1, and sel_value_2 variables. Here is the result if your entry for sel_value_2 matches sel.

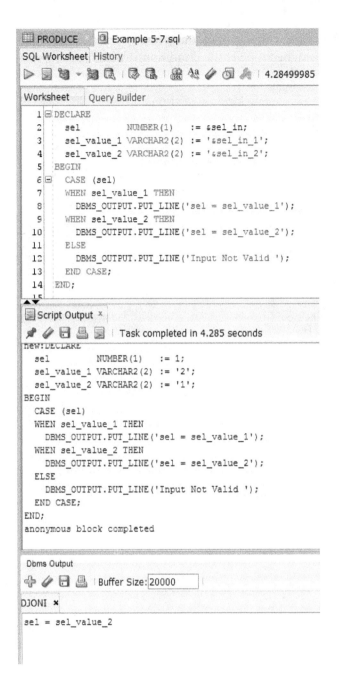

Searched CASE

A Searched CASE statement has the following syntax.

```
CASE
WHEN condition_1 THEN statements_1
WHEN condition_2 THEN statements_2
WHEN...
ELSE else_statements
END CASE;
```

The searched CASE statement executes the first statement for which its condition is true. Remaining conditions are not evaluated. If no condition is true, the CASE statement runs else_statements if they exist and raises the predefined exception CASE_NOT_FOUND otherwise.

While in the Simple CASE, the "condition" of selecting which statements to execute is comparing the selection_value to the selector for equality, in Searched CASE the condition is within each WHEN.

The conditions are independent; they do not need to have any kind of relationship.

Two or more conditions can be true, but only the first in the order you have in the source program (top to bottom) will be granted and its statements executed.

Please run the following SQL TRUNCATE statement to delete all rows from the produce table.

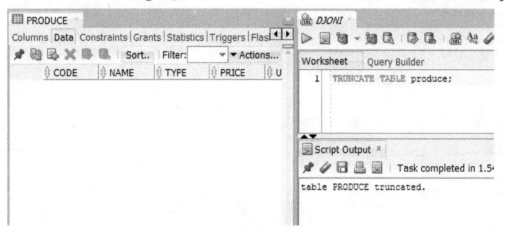

Then, add the initial five rows.

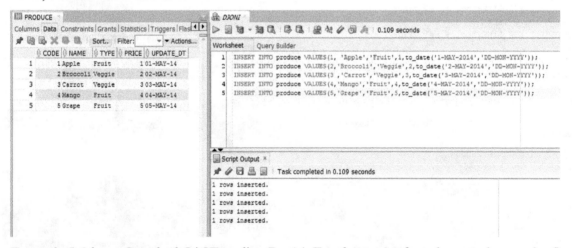

Example 5-8 has a Searched CASE on line 7 – 14. For the rows of produce as shown, the first condition is false and the second condition is true. As a result of executing the second case statement, the prices get updated, and the produce table will then be as shown here.

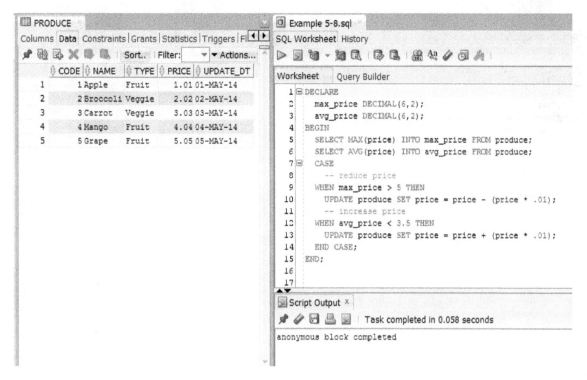

Basic LOOP

The structure of the Basic LOOP is

```
<<label>> LOOP
statements
END LOOP;
```

The statements run from the first to the last before the END LOOP, and then back to the first, until an EXIT conditional statement, which should be provided within the loop, is satisfied on which the loop is terminated.

The label is optional, but it helps clarifies the scope of the loop.

The loop in Example 5-9 iterates statements on line 9 – 10 three times. On the fourth iteration num = 4, hence the exit condition is satisfied, the next statement after the loop on line 13 is executed, and then the program ends.

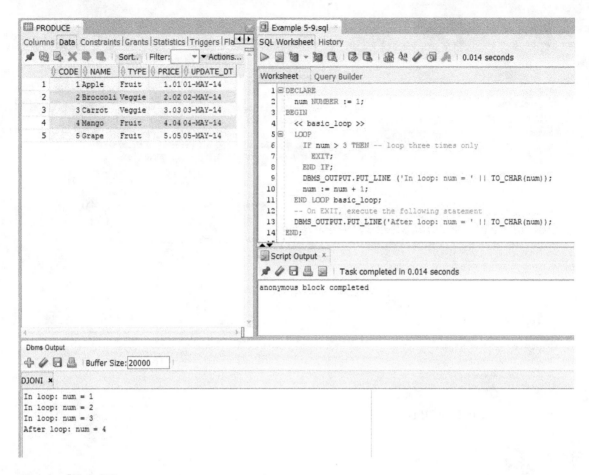

Nested LOOP

You can nest a loop. In Example 5-10 the inner loop on line 10 - 15 is nested within the outer loop that starts on line 5. For each iteration of the outer loop, the inner loop is iterated twice.

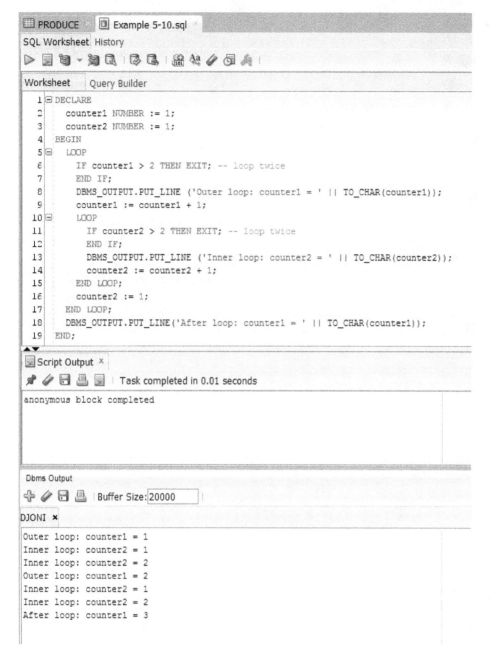

Fixed Iteration

If you know exactly the number of iteration, you can use the following loop structure.

```
FOR i IN l..u
  LOOP
    statements;
  END LOOP;
```

i the loop index, l the lower bound and u is the upper bound of the index. The index value starts with l when the loop is entered, and increments by 1; the last iteration is when the index reaches u.

In Example 5-11, the dbms_output.put_line statement inside the loop is executed three times as for this example i= 1 and u = 3.

WHILE loop

You can also use a WHILE to form a loop. Its syntax is as follows.

```
WHILE condition LOOP
statements;
END LOOP;
```

The statements in the loop will be executed as long as the condition is true. You must ensure the loop can terminate.

Example 5-12 does the same as Example 5-11; its loop terminates when i = 4. Notice that the i variable used here must be declared; while with LOOP as in Example 5-11 should not be. The i variable is incremented on line 6, which will terminate the loop when its value reaches 4.

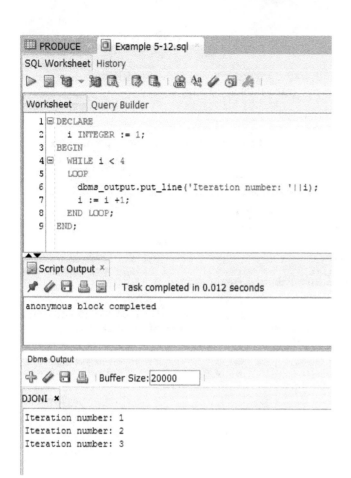

```
  1  DECLARE
  2     i INTEGER := 1;
  3  BEGIN
  4     WHILE i < 4
  5     LOOP
  6        dbms_output.put_line('Iteration number: '||i);
  7        i := i +1;
  8     END LOOP;
  9  END;
```

Script Output ×

Task completed in 0.012 seconds

anonymous block completed

Dbms Output

Buffer Size: 20000

DJONI ×

Iteration number: 1
Iteration number: 2
Iteration number: 3

Chapter 6: Exception-handling

If a program runs into a problem, it will abort; the program fails at run-time.

Please truncate the produce table and insert the five initial rows.

Example 6.1 fails on the SELECT query. The query does not return any row, as the produce table does not have any Pineapple. The program is aborted.

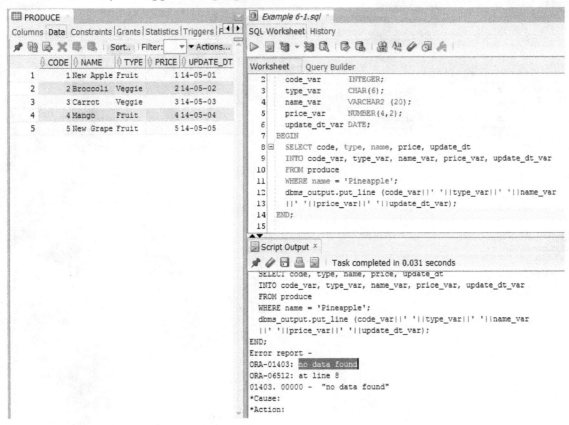

The syntax of an exception handler statement is:

```
WHEN exception THEN exception-handler statements
```

In Example 6.2, when the program encounters a no_data_found exception, its dbm_output.put_line exception-handling statement is executed; the program gets completed successfully.

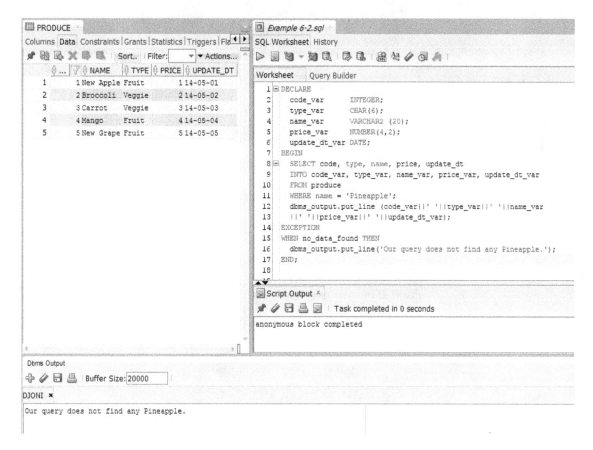

Multiple Exception-handling Statement

An Exception part can have more than one statement.

The Exception part of Example 6-3 has **two** statements. Any error that is not too_many_rows is handled by the OTHERS statement. The error encounters by this program is caused by the query that does not return any row, hence this error is handled by the OTHERS handler. (The OTHERS exception is used for catch-all other types of error not caught by other specific exception handlers.)

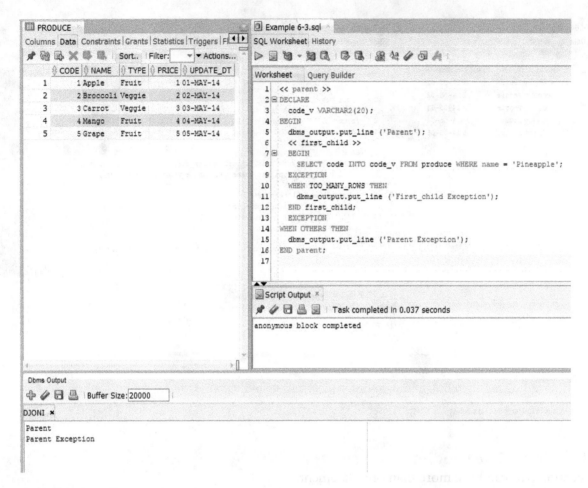

Combining Exceptions

If you want the same exception action for different exception-handlers, you can put them into one exception. The syntax is then as follows.

```
WHEN exception1 OR exception2 OR…
THEN exception_action
```

Example 6-4 has one exception with two handlers.

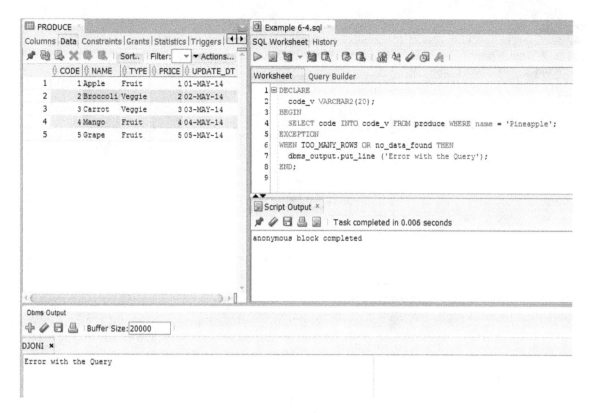

Visibility of Exception

Similar to the scope of a variable, an exception handler in a nested block is visible only within itself. On the other hand a parents' exception handlers can handle its children's exceptions if they do not have the applicable handlers.

In Example 6.5 the parent's query on line 6 does not return any row. It does not have any no_data_found exception handler. As the first_child's no_data_found exception is not visible to the parent, the program will fail.

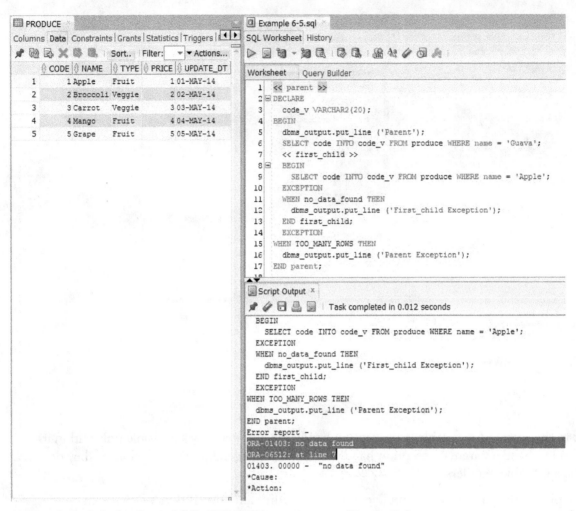

In Example 6.6, the first_child's SELECT statement on line 8 -9 does not return any row, as it does not have DATA_NOT_FOUND exception handler, its parent's no_data_found exception handles this exception.

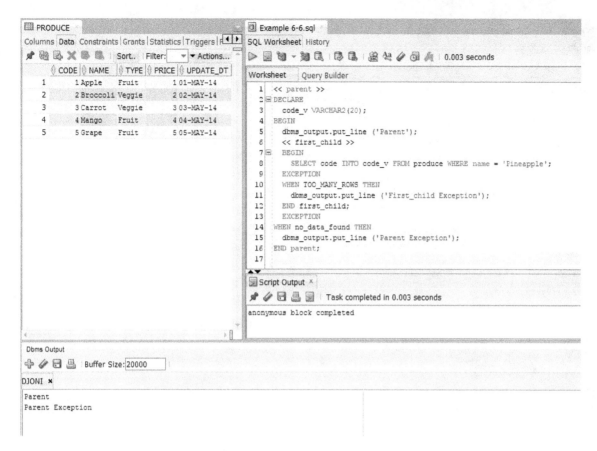

Predefined Exceptions

NO_DATA_FOUND and OTHERS that we already used in the examples far are two of the PL/SQL predefined exceptions.

VALUE_ERROR is another example of predefined exception. Example 6.7 uses this predefined exception. Line 4 tries to assign a string of six characters, which is longer than the maximum length specified for the x variable. The VALUE_ERROR exception handler on line 7 - 9 catches this error.

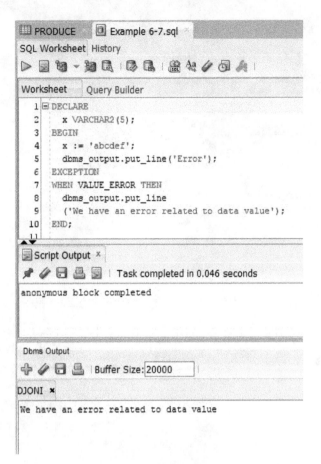

Please consult the Oracle PL/SQL manual for a complete list of the predefined exceptions.

SQLCODE and SQLERRM functions

PL/SQL provides SQLCODE and SQLERRM functions; when you call these functions, they will return the Oracle error code and message respectively for the error encountered by your program at run time.

Example 6-8 demonstrates the use of the two functions on line 7 and 8.

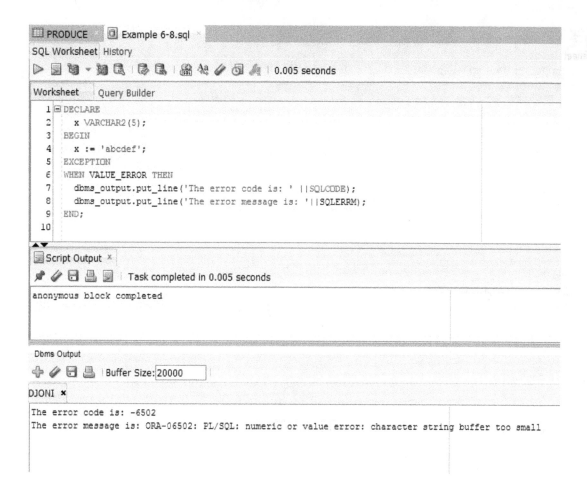

Defining Oracle Error

You might have an error that does not have a pre-defined exception. Fortunately, PL/SQL has a feature to solve it known as PRAGMA EXCEPTION_INIT. You first declare an EXCEPTION in the Declaration part; its syntax is as follows.

```
exception EXCEPTION;
```

Then, also in the Declaration part, you define that exception with the following syntax.

```
PRAGMA EXCEPTION_INIT(exception, -Oracle_error_number);
```

where `exception_name` is the name of the exception you already declare, and the number is a negative value corresponding to an `ORA-` error number. You will need to find out this error number in the Oracle manual, or find it using the SQLCODE function we discussed in the previous section (Example 6-8)

In Example 6-9 the UPDATE tries to update a primary key to an existing value causing an exception. The error number for violating unique constraint violation is -1.

User Defined Exception

All previous exceptions were run-time errors. You can also define your own exceptions that are not run-time errors, and let the Exception part handle these user-defined exceptions in the same fashion as run-time error exceptions.

In Example 6-10, we want any price higher than 4.5 as an exception, hence we declare it on line 7. We then use it within the IF THEN statement in on line 13 – 14 as the target of a RAISE statement (RAISE is a reserved word). The Exception part must have a handler for the exception as shown on line 17 – 18.

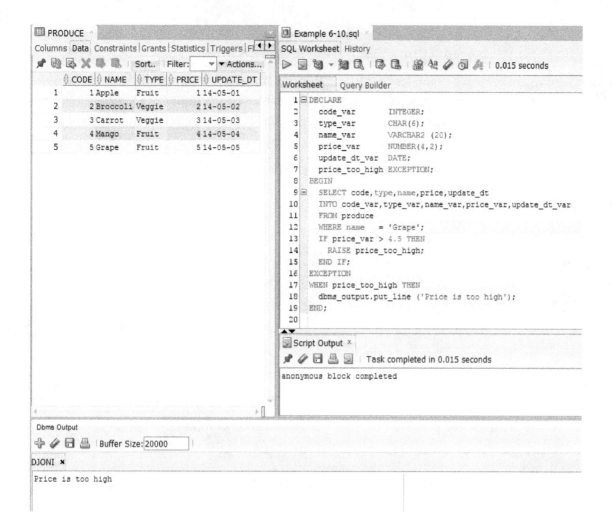

PRODUCE

Columns | Data | Constraints | Grants | Statistics | Triggers | F

Sort.. | Filter: | ▼ Actions...

	CODE	NAME	TYPE	PRICE	UPDATE_DT
1	1	Apple	Fruit	1	14-05-01
2	2	Broccoli	Veggie	2	14-05-02
3	3	Carrot	Veggie	3	14-05-03
4	4	Mango	Fruit	4	14-05-04
5	5	Grape	Fruit	5	14-05-05

Example 6-10.sql

SQL Worksheet | History

0.015 seconds

Worksheet | Query Builder

```
 1  DECLARE
 2      code_var        INTEGER;
 3      type_var        CHAR(6);
 4      name_var        VARCHAR2 (20);
 5      price_var       NUMBER(4,2);
 6      update_dt_var   DATE;
 7      price_too_high EXCEPTION;
 8  BEGIN
 9      SELECT code, type, name, price, update_dt
10      INTO code_var, type_var, name_var, price_var, update_dt_var
11      FROM produce
12      WHERE name   = 'Grape';
13      IF price_var > 4.5 THEN
14        RAISE price_too_high;
15      END IF;
16  EXCEPTION
17  WHEN price_too_high THEN
18      dbms_output.put_line ('Price is too high');
19  END;
20
```

Script Output ×

Task completed in 0.015 seconds

anonymous block completed

Dbms Output

Buffer Size: 20000

DJONI ×

Price is too high

Chapter 7: Using SQL in PL/SQL

You have seen in the previous examples that PL/SQL programs can have both *procedural statements* and *SQL statements*. In this chapter we will focus on the SQL statements used in PL/SQL programs.

The purpose of Example 7-1 is to increase price by 10% of the average price, on those prices lower than average unit price.

The program has two SQL statements, a SELECT statement and an UPDATE statement.

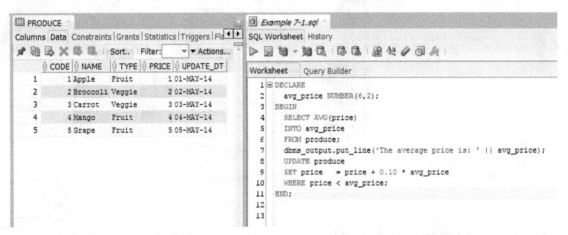

When you run the program, the prices on the produce table will be as follows.

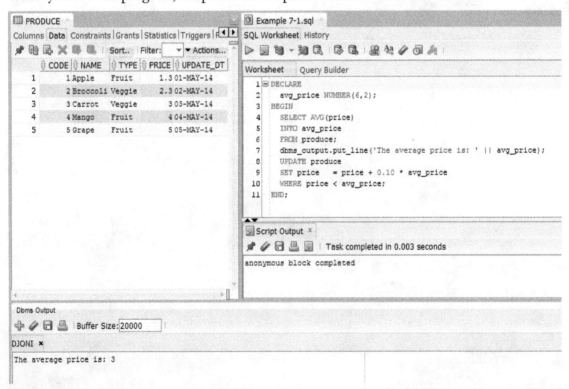

PL/SQL Advantage over SQL's

When you run a PL/SQL program, such as Example 7-1, all lines of statements are sent to the database at once. All SQL statements will be sent together. All results will also be sent back once, such as all output displays by the dbms_output.put_line back to the SQL Developer. Such PL/SQL program with more than one SQL statement will likely be executed faster than submitting one statement after another.

INTO clause

Note that the SELECT statement must have an INTO clause, which is applicable only within PL/SQL programs.

The SELECT with INTO syntax is

```
SELECT select_columns INTO into_columns FROM ...
```

The into_columns must be in the sequence and the same datatype as those of the select_columns. Example 7-2 has a SELECT statement that has three INTO columns.

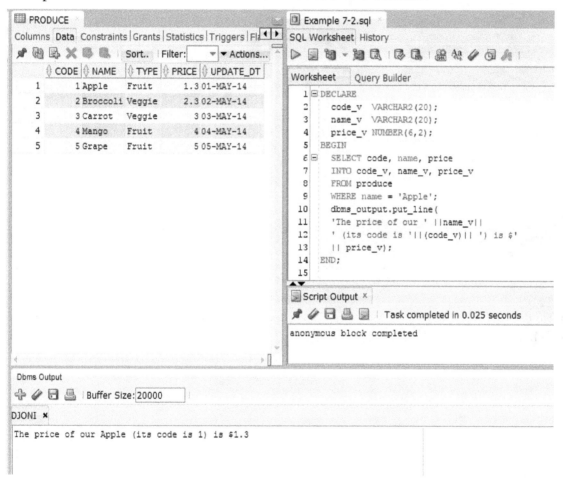

Only One Row

A SELECT INTO must return exactly one row.

Example 7-3 fails as its query returns more than one row.

```
Example 7-3.sql
SQL Worksheet  History

Worksheet   Query Builder
  1 □ DECLARE
  2     code_v  VARCHAR2(20);
  3     name_v  VARCHAR2(20);
  4     price_v NUMBER(6,2);
  5   BEGIN
  6     SELECT code, name, price
  7     INTO code_v, name_v, price_v
  8     FROM produce;
  9     dbms_output.put_line(
 10     'The price of our ' ||name_v||
 11     ' (its code is '||(code_v)|| ') is $'
 12     || price_v);
 13   END;
 14
```

Script Output ×

Task completed in 0.058 seconds

```
  SELECT code, name, price
  INTO code_v, name_v, price_v
  FROM produce;
  dbms_output.put_line(
  'The price of our ' ||name_v||
  ' (its code is '||(code_v)|| ') is $'
  || price_v);
END;
Error report -
ORA-01422: exact fetch returns more than requested number of rows
ORA-06512: at line 6
01422. 00000 -  "exact fetch returns more than requested number of rows"
*Cause:     The number specified in exact fetch is less than the rows returned.
*Action:    Rewrite the query or change number of rows requested
```

You can use the PL/SQL predefined too_many_rows exception to handle this error as shown in Example 7-4.

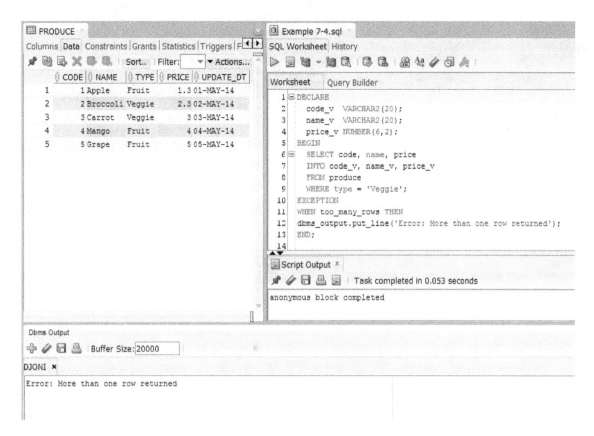

ROWTYPE and TYPE

PL/SQL provides two special datatypes to make sure the variables you use as the INTO columns are correctly the same as the table's columns. The syntax of the ROWTYPE and TYPE datatypes syntaxes are respectively:

```
variable_name table_name%ROWTYPE;
variable_name column_name%TYPE;
```

You use ROWTYPE to at once refer to all the columns of the table; while the TYPE refers to a specific column.

Example 7-5 uses these two datatypes. The avg_price has the unit_price column's datatype of the produce table. The p_row consists of columns that match the produce table's columns; for example, the first column, p_row.code has the same datatype as that of produce.code. Note the use of dot notation to refer to a column.

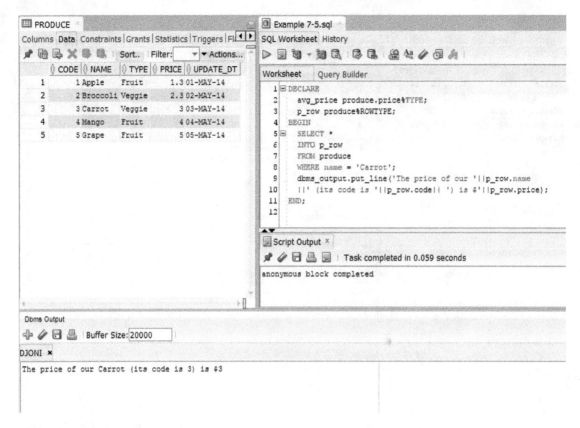

SELECT for UPDATE

When you need to first SELECT and then UPDATE the selected row, and you want to be sure the selected row is not updated by any other SQL statement while you are updating it, you can lock the selected row using a SELECT for UPDATE statement as demonstrated in Example 7-6.

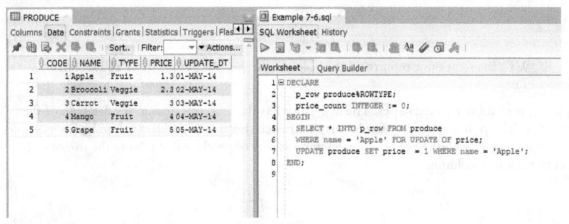

When you run the program, the Apple's price will be updated to 1.

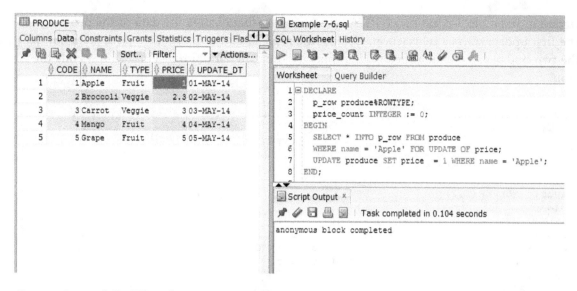

Commit and Rollback

A COMMIT statement commits new, deleted and updates rows persistently in the database. You can issue a ROLLBACK statement to back out changes that have not been committed.

Example 7-7 has both the COMMIT and ROLLBACK statements. The update to the Apple's price is committed if it is the only produce with 1.5 price (which is true); otherwise, the update is roll-backed.

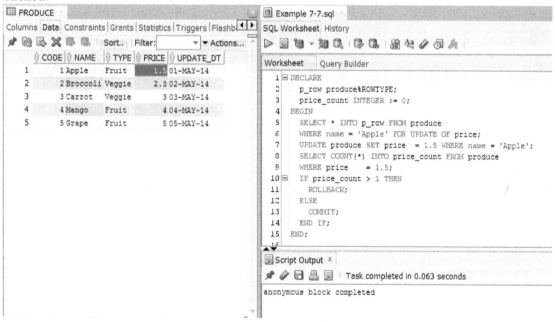

Note that your program can also have a DELETE statement.

Transaction

A transaction is a group of SQL statements. You control the grouped statements so that the data changes they have effected are committed (applied to the database persistently) using a COMMIT statement, or rolled back (undone from the database) using a ROLLBACK statement.

The program in Example 7-8 has two UPDATE statements that change the data of the produce table. The first update starts a transaction. If, after the price updates, the average price is higher than 10.00, the two updates would be rolled back; otherwise they are committed. The commit ends the transaction.

```
Example 7-8.sql
Worksheet    Query Builder
 1  --Example 7-8
 2  DECLARE
 3    avgprc NUMBER(6,2);
 4  BEGIN
 5    SELECT AVG(price) INTO avgprc FROM produce;
 6    UPDATE produce SET price = price + (price * 0.10) WHERE price < avgprc;
 7    UPDATE produce SET price = price + (price * 0.01) WHERE price > avgprc;
 8    SELECT AVG(price) INTO avgprc FROM produce;
 9    IF avgprc > 10.00 THEN
10      ROLLBACK;
11    END IF;
12    COMMIT;
13  END;
```

Savepoint

Within a transaction you can set a savepoint to set the boundary of a rollback. In Example 7-9 we set a savepoint named after_insert after the INSERT statement. When a rollback occurs the changes rolled back to only right before the SAVEPOINT statement, i.e. only the insert is roll backed, first update is not

```
Example 7-9.sql
SQL Worksheet  History
Worksheet    Query Builder
 1  DECLARE
 2    avgprc NUMBER(6,2);
 3  BEGIN
 4    SELECT AVG(price) INTO avgprc FROM produce;
 5    UPDATE produce SET price = price + (price * 0.10) WHERE price < avgprc;
 6    INSERT
 7    INTO produce VALUES
 8      (
 9        999,'Kale',
10        'v', 1.50,
11        to_date('1-5-2013','DD-MM-YYYY')
12      );
13    SAVEPOINT after_insert;
14    UPDATE produce SET price = price + (price * 0.01) WHERE price > avgprc;
15    SELECT AVG(price) INTO avgprc FROM produce;
16    IF avgprc > 2.00 THEN
17      ROLLBACK TO after_insert;
18    END IF;
19    COMMIT;
20  END;
```

Multiple Transactions

A program can have more than one transaction. You start a transaction by issuing a SET TRANSACTION statement and end it by a COMMIT or ROLLBACK statement.

The SET TRANSACTION has the following syntax.

SET TRANSACTION *'transaction'*;

The program in Example 7-10 has two transactions: t1 and t2 When the rollback happens, the changes rolled back is only within t2.

```
Example 7-10.sql
SQL Worksheet History

Worksheet   Query Builder
 1  --Example 7-10
 2  DECLARE
 3    avgprc NUMBER(6,2);
 4  BEGIN
 5    SET TRANSACTION NAME 't1';
 6    INSERT
 7    INTO produce VALUES
 8      (
 9        9,'Mellon',
10        'F', 5.50,
11        to_date('1-5-2013','DD-MM-YYYY')
12      );
13    COMMIT;
14    SET TRANSACTION NAME 't2';
15    UPDATE produce SET price = price + (price * 0.10) WHERE price > avgprc;
16    SELECT AVG(price) INTO avgprc FROM produce;
17    IF avgprc > 12.00 THEN
18      ROLLBACK;
19    END IF;
20    COMMIT;
21  END;
```

DDL (Data Definition Language)

All the above SQL statements are DML statements (Data Manipulation Language). You can also have DDL statements in PL/SQL.

Inside a PL/SQL program, you use the EXECUTE IMMEDIATE statement to pass a DDL statement. The EXECUTE IMMEDIATE statement has the following syntax.

EXECUTE IMMEDIATE ('DDL statement');

Example 7-11 has a CREATE TABLE statement (line 2). When you run the the program, the sample_produce table will be created.

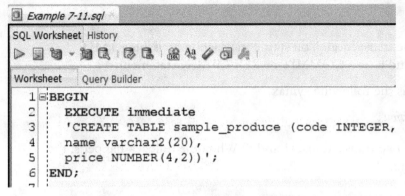

```
Example 7-11.sql

SQL Worksheet  History

Worksheet    Query Builder

1 ⊟BEGIN
2       EXECUTE immediate
3       'CREATE TABLE sample_produce (code INTEGER,
4       name varchar2(20),
5       price NUMBER(4,2))';
6     END;
7
```

Note that the DDL statement is quoted; in the PL/SQL program it is a string literal (value).

Chapter 8: Cursor

A cursor is the storage of **rows** returned by the cursor's query. You define the cursor's **query** when you declare the cursor. The syntax of a declaring a cursor is:

DECLARE CURSOR *cursor_name* IS **query**;

Once a cursor is declared you can use it follows. In the executable part, open the cursor; fetch its rows sequentially, when you are done with the cursor, close it. The syntax of the OPEN, FETCH, and CLOSE statements are respectively:

OPEN *cursor_name*;
FETCH *cursor_name* INTO *variables*;
CLOSE *cursor_name*;

The INTO **variables** clause in the FETCH statement stores the columns of a cursor's row into the **variables**. All data types of the variables must match with the data types of the columns of the rows.

In Example 8-1 a cursor named c_produce is declared on line 2 – 4. Its query returns all rows from the produce table.

To match the data types of the cursor's columns, the v_produce variable used on line 8 to store the cursor's row is declared as the cursor's row type using the %rowtype data typing (see also **Chapter 10: Records,** for other rowtype kinds of data type).

Please truncate the produce table and insert the five initial rows.

When you run Example 8.1, as the FETCH is executed only once only the first row is fetched and displayed.

```
Example 8-1.sql
▷ 🗐 🗐 ▼ 🗐 🗐  🗐 🗐  🗐 🗐  🗐 🗐 ✎ 🗐 🗐   0 seconds
Worksheet    Query Builder
  1  -- Example 8-1
  2  DECLARE
  3    CURSOR c_produce
  4    IS
  5      SELECT * FROM produce;
  6    v_produce c_produce% rowtype;
  7  BEGIN
  8    OPEN c_produce;
  9    FETCH c_produce INTO v_produce;
 10    dbms_output.put_line( v_produce.code || ' '||v_produce.name);
 11    CLOSE c_produce;
 12  END;
 13

Dbms Output
➕ ✎ 🗐 🖨   Buffer Size: 20000
DJONI-XE ✕
1 Apple
```

Cursor Parameters

A cursor can have parameters in its query. Our c_produce cursor in Example 8-1 now has a low_price and high_price parameters (line…). We pass values to the parameters when we open the cursor (line …)

```
Example 8-1.1.sql
SQL Worksheet  History
▷ 🗐 🗐 ▼ 🗐 🗐  🗐 🗐  🗐 🗐 ✎ 🗐 🗐
Worksheet    Query Builder
  1  DECLARE
  2    CURSOR c_produce (c_lowprice NUMBER, c_highprice NUMBER)
  3    IS
  4      SELECT * FROM produce WHERE price BETWEEN c_lowprice AND c_highprice;
  5    v_produce c_produce%rowtype;
  6  BEGIN
  7    OPEN c_produce (2, 4);
  8    FETCH c_produce INTO v_produce;
  9    dbms_output.put_line( v_produce.code ||' '||v_produce.name ||' '|| v_produce.price);
 10    CLOSE c_produce;
 11  END;
```

PL/SQL Variable in the Query

A cursor's query can include PL/SQL variable.

The cursor's query in Example 8.2 uses price_increase variable in its second output column. This column is added to the produce's unit_price; the sum is aliased as new_price.

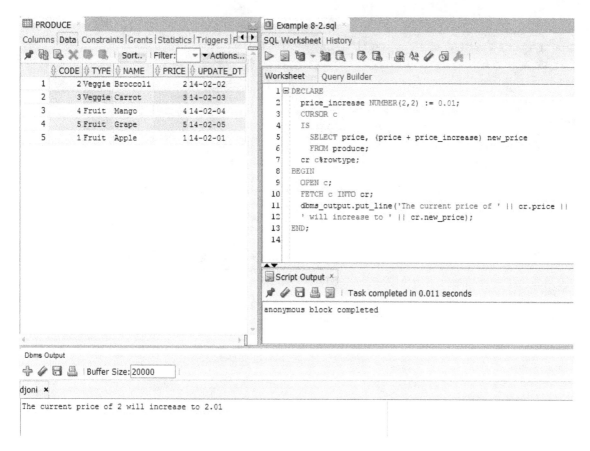

Cursor Last Row

Fetching beyond the last row does not produce any error, the value in the INTO variable is still that from last rows fetched.

Example 8.3 will be completed successfully. The loop iterates six times. As the produce table has five rows only and code 1 is the last code fetched, the 5th and the 6th outputs are 1.

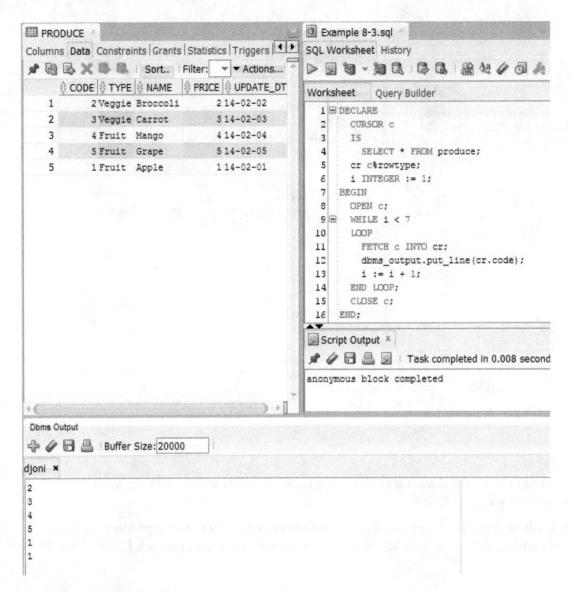

Cursor Attributes

PL/SQL provides %ISOPEN, %FOUND, %NOTFOUND, and %ROWCOUNT attributes.

As you will not generally know in advance the number of rows in a cursor, you don't know when to stop the loop iteration. Fortunately you can use the %notfound cursor attribute to detect when there is no more row in a cursor. In Example 8.4, the "EXIT WHEN %notfound" statement (line 10 - 11) stops the loop from fetching further beyond the last row.

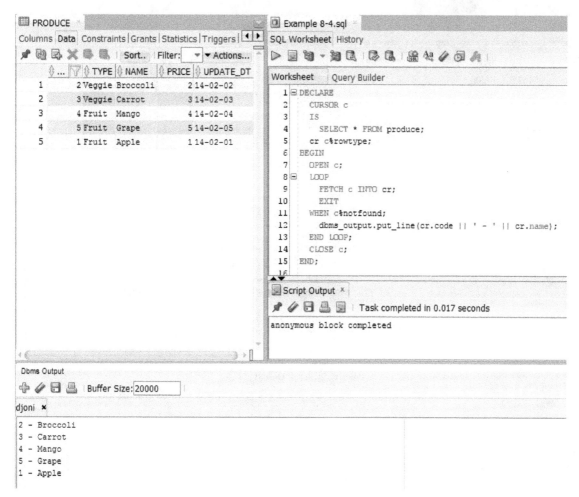

The use of the %isopen attribute is demonstrated in Example 8.5. The c cursor queries the name column from the produce table and stores it into name_c variable. As the name_c variable is too short to store the name, an exception occurs. The exception is handled by the WHEN OTHERS. Line 13 uses the %isopen to check the status of the c cursor and finds that the cursor is still open, hence it is closed.

Note that the dbms_output.put_line can only display string. As %isopen has a Boolean datatype, we use the s variable to store the string message conveying the cursor open status that we want to display.

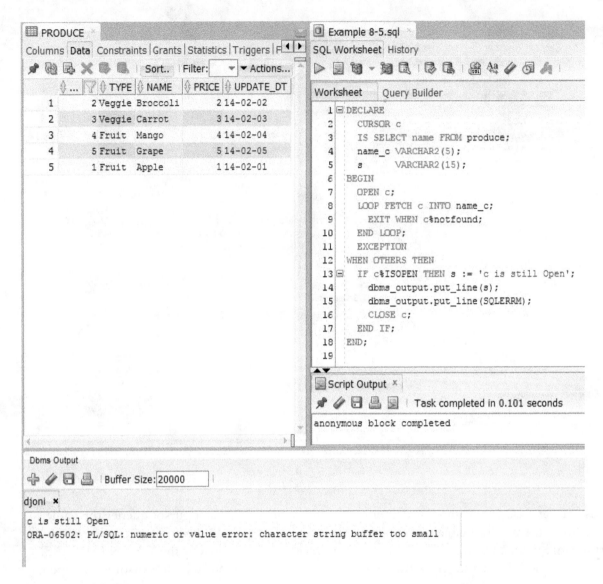

Cursor FOR Loop

The cursor FOR loop specifies a sequence of statements to be repeated once for each row returned by a cursor. Use the cursor FOR loop if you need to process every record from a cursor; it does not need you to open, fetch and close the cursor.

In Example 8.6, using the c_index (a variable that you don't need to declare), the for-loop on line 9 – 12, displays the code and name of every produce from the cursor.

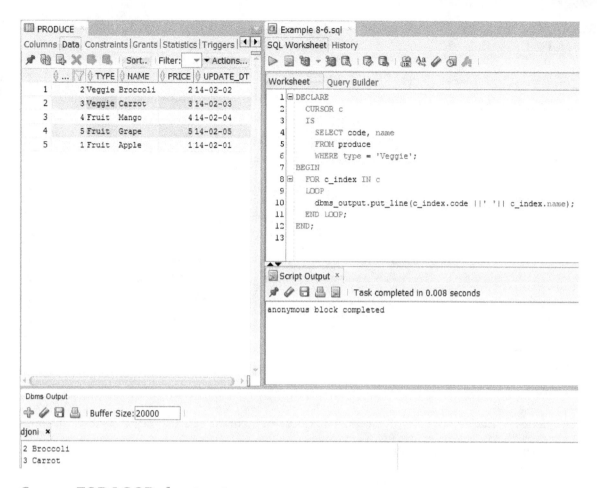

Cursor FOR LOOP short cut

A statement with the following syntax effectively loops through the rows returned by the query.

```
FOR returned_rows IN
(query)
LOOP
   statements;
END LOOP;
```

No cursor is declared. You don't need to declare the returned_rows which stores the query's returned rows. The loop iterates through all rows returned by the query.

In Example 8.7 all rows from the produce table are returned. These rows are all processed one by one sequentially. Each of the output string, the produce's type and name, to be displayed is constructed on line 7.

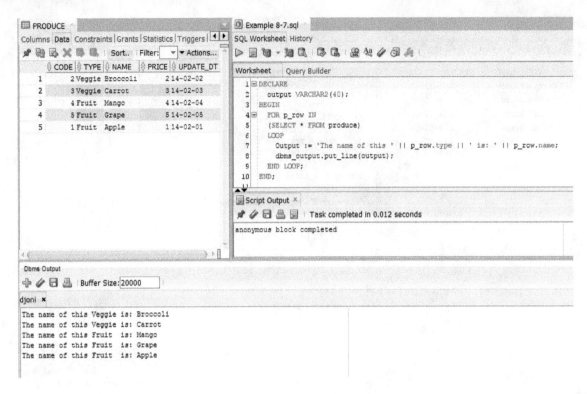

View

So far, the queries of our cursors are on tables. The query of a cursor can also be on a view.

Assume we have a view, produce_v, created using the CREATE VIEW statement as follows.

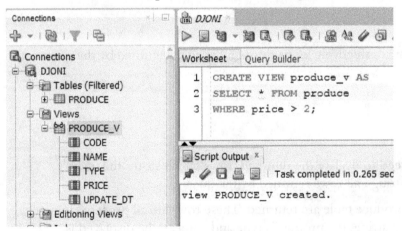

The cursor-for-loop in Example 8.8, line 4 – 11, has a query that uses the produce_v view you have just created.

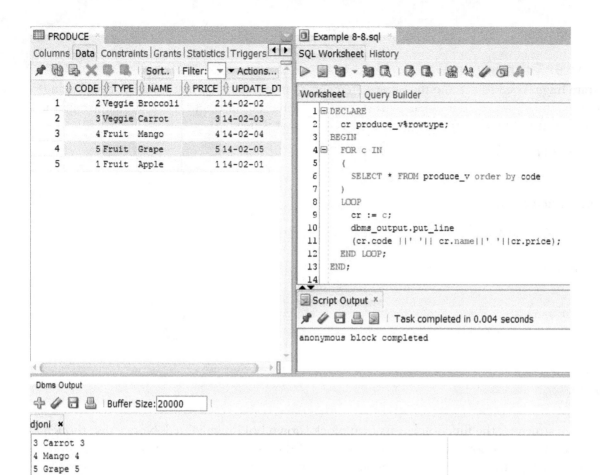

PRODUCE

Columns | **Data** | Constraints | Grants | Statistics | Triggers ◀ ▶

📌 📲 📤 ✖ 📰 📑 | Sort.. | Filter: ▼ ▼ Actions...

	CODE	TYPE	NAME	PRICE	UPDATE_DT
1	2	Veggie	Broccoli	2	14-02-02
2	3	Veggie	Carrot	3	14-02-03
3	4	Fruit	Mango	4	14-02-04
4	5	Fruit	Grape	5	14-02-05
5	1	Fruit	Apple	1	14-02-01

Example 8-8.sql

SQL Worksheet History

▷ 📋 📒 ▾ 📒 📖 | 📒 📖 | 📖 🗚 ✎ 📄 🔍

Worksheet | Query Builder

```
 1 □ DECLARE
 2      cr produce_v%rowtype;
 3   BEGIN
 4 □   FOR c IN
 5       (
 6         SELECT * FROM produce_v order by code
 7       )
 8       LOOP
 9         cr := c;
10         dbms_output.put_line
11         (cr.code ||' '|| cr.name||' '||cr.price);
12       END LOOP;
13   END;
14
```

Script Output ×

📌 ✎ 💾 🖨 📋 | Task completed in 0.004 seconds

anonymous block completed

Dbms Output

➕ ✎ 💾 🖨 | Buffer Size: 20000

djoni ×

```
3 Carrot 3
4 Mango 4
5 Grape 5
```

Chapter 9: Subprogram

A program might need to execute the same statements in more than one place. Rather than having the same statements repeated in those places, you can define the statements once as a subprogram. You can then just call the subprogram in the places where it is needed.

Subprogram can be a function or a procedure.

Function

A function when called returns a value.

In the Declaration part of the program you specify the function using the following structure.

```
DECLARE
  FUNCTION function (parameters)
    RETURN data_type
  IS
    variables; -- if any is needed in the Executable part
    BEGIN
    Executable statements; -- what the function does
    RETURN value; -- you can have more than one RETURN
    EXCEPTION
    Exception_handlers;
    END function;
```

In the above structure, the function has its own block shown bold-highlighted. Notice that though the function block does not have its own DECLARE, if the function need any variable you can declare the variables after the IS reserved word. The value of the RETURN statement is returned (produced) when the function is called.

Example 9-1 is a program that has a function named *uc_name*. The function converts and returns the name of a produce in uppercase.

You identify the produce by specifying its code in the parameter of the function. The parameter *code_p* has the datatype of the produce's code column.

The SELECT statement (line 9 – 12) retrieves the produce name that has its code = code_p. The produce name converted to uppercase is stored into the name_uc variable.

When the function encounters any error during its run time, its OTHERS exception handler's returns an 'Error'.

You call the function as follows: uc_name (*code_p*).

The function is called twice, first on line 23, then on line 26. The first call is in the loop. The dbms_output.put_line in the loop produces the list of all produce names in uppercase. The second call tests if produce code 9 exists in the table; if it does not, 'Error' will be displayed.

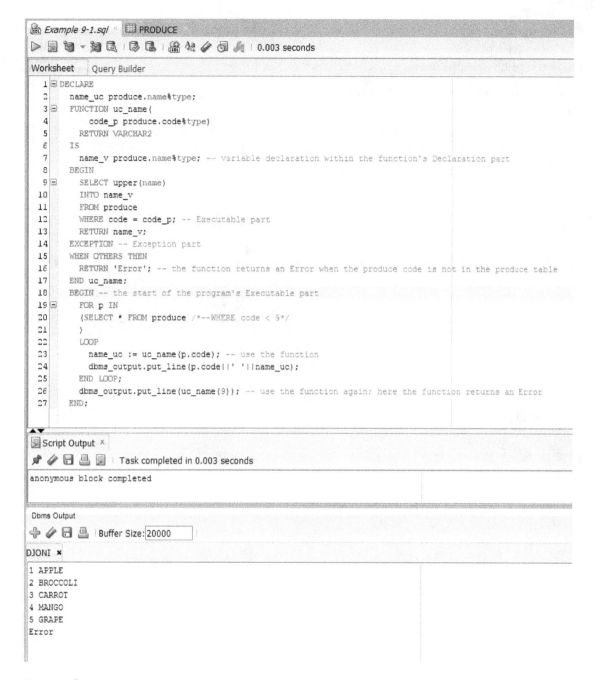

```
1  ⊟ DECLARE
2       name_uc produce.name%type;
3  ⊟    FUNCTION uc_name(
4            code_p produce.code%type)
5         RETURN VARCHAR2
6       IS
7         name_v produce.name%type; -- variable declaration within the function's Declaration part
8       BEGIN
9  ⊟      SELECT upper(name)
10         INTO name_v
11         FROM produce
12         WHERE code = code_p; -- Executable part
13         RETURN name_v;
14      EXCEPTION -- Exception part
15      WHEN OTHERS THEN
16         RETURN 'Error'; -- the function returns an Error when the produce code is not in the produce table
17      END uc_name;
18      BEGIN -- the start of the program's Executable part
19 ⊟      FOR p IN
20         (SELECT * FROM produce /*--WHERE code < 9*/
21         )
22         LOOP
23           name_uc := uc_name(p.code); -- use the function
24           dbms_output.put_line(p.code||' '||name_uc);
25         END LOOP;
26         dbms_output.put_line(uc_name(9)); -- use the function again; here the function returns an Error
27      END;
```

Script Output ×

Task completed in 0.003 seconds

anonymous block completed

Dbms Output

Buffer Size: 20000

DJONI ×

```
1 APPLE
2 BROCCOLI
3 CARROT
4 MANGO
5 GRAPE
Error
```

Procedure

While a function returns a value, a procedure does some actions. Here is the structure of a procedure.

```
DECLARE
  PROCEDURE procedure (parameters)
  IS
    variables; -- if any is needed in the Executable part
  BEGIN
    statements; -- what the function does
  END procedure;
```

The procedure update_price in Example 9-2 takes the name of a produce as a parameter and increase the produce's price by 10%. The Executable part uses the procedure twice, on line 12 and 13, to update the price of Apple and Carrot.

You call the procedure as follows: update_price (*name*).

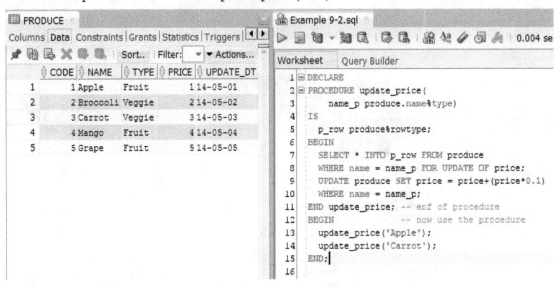

When you finish running Example 9-2, the prices of Apple and Carrot are as seen here.

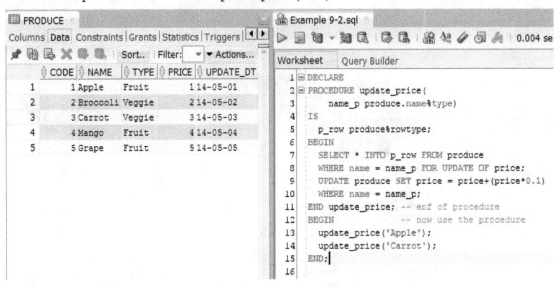

Stored Programs

The previous function and procedure are in-line; they are defined, and at the same time used, in the same programs.

You can also create them so they are stored in the database as database objects. You can then use them in any other program.

To create stored function and procedure you use the CREATE FUNCTION and CREATE PROCEDURE statements that have the following syntaxes respectively.

Example 9.3 and 9.4 show the statements to create the stored versions of our uc_name function and update_price procedure. When you run these CREATE statements the uc_name function and update_price procedure will be created and stored in the database.

```
Example 9-3.sql
SQL Worksheet   History

Worksheet    Query Builder
 1 CREATE FUNCTION uc_name(
 2      cp_code produce.code%type)
 3    RETURN VARCHAR2
 4  IS
 5    v_name produce.name%type;
 6  BEGIN
 7    SELECT upper(name) INTO v_name FROM produce WHERE code = cp_code;
 8    RETURN v_name;
 9  EXCEPTION
10  WHEN OTHERS THEN
11    RETURN 'Error';
12  END uc_name;
13
```

```
Example 9-4.sql

Worksheet    Query Builder
 1 CREATE PROCEDURE update_price(
 2      cp_name produce.name%type)
 3  AS
 4    v_produce produce%rowtype;
 5  BEGIN
 6    SELECT * INTO v_produce FROM produce WHERE name = cp_name FOR UPDATE OF price;
 7    UPDATE produce SET price = price+(price*0.1) WHERE name = cp_name;
 8  END update_price;
```

Example 9.5 and 9.6 are programs that use the stored function and procedure
respectively. These programs are effectively the same as that in the Executable part of
Example 9.1 and 9.2.

```
Example 9-5.sql

Worksheet    Query Builder
 1 DECLARE
 2      v_name produce.name%type;
 3  BEGIN
 4    FOR p IN
 5    (SELECT * FROM produce
 6    )
 7    LOOP
 8      v_name:=un_name(p.code);
 9      dbms_output.put_line(p.code||' '||v_name);
10    END LOOP;
11  END;
```

```
Example 9-6.sql
SQL Worksheet  History

Worksheet    Query Builder
  1 ⊟ BEGIN
  2      update_price('Apple');
  3      update_price('Carrot');
  4   END;
```

Package

We can put together stored procedures and functions into a stored package. The dbms_output.put_line procedure we have been using is one of the built-in packages. Put_line is one of the procedures in the dbms_output package. We access the procedures and function in a package using a dot notation.

A package has two parts: specification and body. The specification declares the procedures and functions in the body.

Creating Package

A package has two parts: specification and body.

The mypackage packages our uc_name function and update_price package. The package specification and body are created by the statements in Example 9-7 and 9-8 respectively.

```
Example 9-7.sql
SQL Worksheet  History

Worksheet    Query Builder
  1 ⊟ CREATE PACKAGE mypackage
  2   AS
  3      FUNCTION uc_name(
  4          cp_code produce.code%type)
  5        RETURN VARCHAR2;
  6      PROCEDURE update_price(
  7          cp_name produce.name%type);
  8   END mypackage;
  9
```

Example 9-8.sql

```
SQL Worksheet  History

▷ ▤ ▦ ▾ ▨ ▨  ▨ ▨  ▦ ▨ ▨ ▨ ▨ ▨        ▨ local

Worksheet    Query Builder
 1 ⊟ CREATE PACKAGE body mypackage
 2   AS
 3 ⊟   FUNCTION uc_name(
 4          cp_code produce.code%type)
 5       RETURN VARCHAR2
 6     IS
 7       name_v VARCHAR2(50);
 8     BEGIN
 9       SELECT upper(name) INTO name_v FROM produce WHERE code = cp_code;
10       RETURN name_v;
11     EXCEPTION
12     WHEN OTHERS THEN
13       RETURN 'Error';
14     END uc_name;
15 ⊟   PROCEDURE update_price(
16          cp_name produce.name%type)
17     AS
18       v_produce produce%rowtype;
19     BEGIN
20       SELECT * INTO v_produce FROM produce WHERE name = cp_name FOR UPDATE OF price;
21       UPDATE produce SET price = price+(price*0.1) WHERE name = cp_name;
22     END update_price;
23   END mypackage;
```

Trigger

A trigger is a database object that has some PL/SQL codes, which get fired (executed) in response to a specified event. The event can be, for example, a delete, insert, or update statement.

The syntax of the CREATE TRIGGER is as follows.

```
CREATE TRIGGER trigger
BEFORE | AFTER
DELETE | OR INSERT | OR UPDATE
ON table
PL/SQL block
```

The t_prodlog trigger create by Example 9-9 is fired when a delete or insert statement is executed on the produce table.

When the trigger is fired the PL/SQL program (which is simply the INSERT statement in this trigger) is executed before (as we use of the BEFORE clause on the create tstatement), a row with one column, the current date is added into the prodlog table.

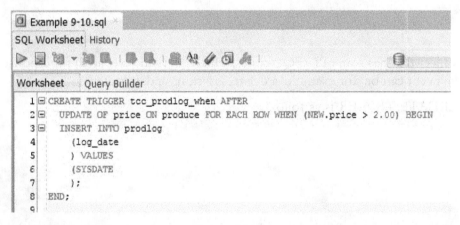

```
Example 9-9.sql
Worksheet    Query Builder
1  CREATE TRIGGER t_prodlog BEFORE
2     DELETE OR
3     INSERT ON produce BEGIN
4     INSERT INTO prodlog
5        (log_date
6        ) VALUES
7        (SYSDATE
8        );
9  END;
```

To test the t_prodlog trigger you need to create the prodlog table. Use the following statement to create the prodlog table.

```
CREATE TABLE prodlog (log_date DATE, p_code VARCHAR2(6));
```

Conditioning the Trigger

You can add a condition restricting when a trigger should fire. The trigger in Example 9-10 has a condition using the FOR EACH ROW WHEN clause. Now, only if the new unit price (that is the unit_price after the update, thanks to the NEW reserve word) is higher than 2.00 the insert will be executed.

```
Example 9-10.sql
SQL Worksheet  History
Worksheet    Query Builder
1  CREATE TRIGGER tcc_prodlog_when AFTER
2     UPDATE OF price ON produce FOR EACH ROW WHEN (NEW.price > 2.00) BEGIN
3     INSERT INTO prodlog
4        (log_date
5        ) VALUES
6        (SYSDATE
7        );
8  END;
```

On top of the WHEN condition, you can further restrict by specifying specific columns on the UPDATE clause. The trigger created by Example 9-11 will only fire when the update is on the unit_price column.

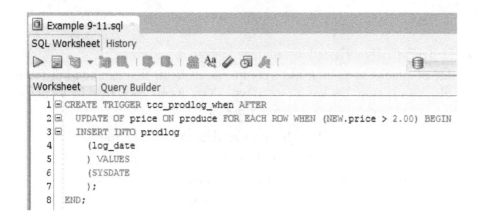

```
Example 9-11.sql
SQL Worksheet History

Worksheet    Query Builder
1 ⊟ CREATE TRIGGER tcc_prodlog_when AFTER
2 ⊟    UPDATE OF price ON produce FOR EACH ROW WHEN (NEW.price > 2.00) BEGIN
3 ⊟    INSERT INTO prodlog
4         (log_date
5         ) VALUES
6         (SYSDATE
7         );
8    END;
```

A trigger can also called stored procedures. Example 9-12 is an example trigger that calls a stored procedure, the increase_price that we created earlier.

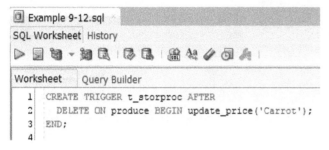

```
Example 9-12.sql
SQL Worksheet History

Worksheet    Query Builder
1   CREATE TRIGGER t_storproc AFTER
2     DELETE ON produce BEGIN update_price('Carrot');
3   END;
4
```

Chapter 10: Records and Collection

A record is like a row outside of a table; as such, it has a composite of fields that can be of different data types. You store records in a variable that has a record type. You access each field by its name qualified by the record name using the dot notation: *record_name.field_name*.

You have used %ROWTYPE to define a variable to have a row data type in Chapter 8. The %ROWTYPE is one of the ways to declare a record type variable.

As a reference, here's again Example 8-2 from Chapter 8. (Shown here as Example 10-1)

```
Example 10-1.sql
SQL Worksheet  History

Worksheet    Query Builder

 1  DECLARE
 2    CURSOR c_produce (c_lowprice NUMBER, c_highprice NUMBER)
 3    IS
 4      SELECT * FROM produce WHERE price BETWEEN c_lowprice AND c_highprice;
 5    v_produce c_produce%rowtype;
 6  BEGIN
 7    OPEN c_produce (2, 4);
 8    FETCH c_produce INTO v_produce;
 9    dbms_output.put_line( v_produce.code ||' '||v_produce.name ||' '|| v_produce.price);
10    CLOSE c_produce;
11  END;
12
```

Using %ROWTYPE is a convenient way to match the fields of records to the columns of table rows; and then, when the column specification changes the field specification automatically gets adjusted accordingly; they are always in sync.

In addition to %ROWTYPE, you can define your own record type.

User-defined Record

To get to a user_defined record is a two-step process. You first define a RECORD type and then declare a variable of that record type.

The syntax to declare a record type is as follows.

```
DECLARE TYPE record_name IS RECORD (field1 datatype, field2 data type, … );
```

When you define your own RECORD type, you can specify a NOT NULL constraint on fields and give them default values.

Example 10-2 demonstrates the use of a user-defined record. This example declares two variables (prod_rec and my_prod) to have the prodtype record type. Notice their use:

Line … reads a row from the produce table into the prod_rec variable and then in line … in just one statement we assign all fields of a record to another record of the same type.

```
Example 10-2.sql

SQL Worksheet  History

▷ 🗐 🗐 ▾ 🗐 🗐 | 🗐 🗐 | 🗐 Aa ✎ 🗐 ᵴ |                           🗐

Worksheet    Query Builder

 1 ⊟ DECLARE
 2    TYPE prodtyp
 3    IS
 4      RECORD
 5      (
 6        prodname  VARCHAR2(30) NOT NULL := 'initial value',
 7        prodprice NUMBER,
 8        prodgroup produce.p_group%TYPE);
 9      prod_rec prodtyp;
10      my_prod prodtyp;
11    BEGIN
12      SELECT name, price, p_group INTO prod_rec FROM produce WHERE code=1;
13      my_prod := prod_rec;
14      dbms_output.put_line(my_prod.prodname||' '||my_prod.prodprice);
15    END;
16
```

Record as Function's Parameter and Return Data Type

You can use record type as function's parameter as well its return data type as shown highlighted in Example 10-3.

Example 10-3.sql

```
SQL Worksheet  History

Worksheet    Query Builder
  1  DECLARE
  2    TYPE prodtyp
  3    IS
  4      RECORD
  5      (
  6        prodname   VARCHAR2(30) NOT NULL := 'initial value',
  7        prodprice NUMBER,
  8        prodgroup produce.p_group%TYPE);
  9      prod_rec prodtyp;
 10      my_prod prodtyp;
 11      rec prodtyp;
 12  FUNCTION frec(
 13        fp_prod_rec prodtyp)
 14      RETURN prodtyp
 15    IS
 16    BEGIN
 17      SELECT name,
 18        price,
 19        p_group
 20      INTO prod_rec
 21      FROM produce
 22      WHERE name = fp_prod_rec.prodname;
 23      my_prod    := prod_rec;
 24      RETURN my_prod;
 25  END frec;
 26  BEGIN
 27    rec.prodname   := 'Carrot';
 28    rec.prodprice := NULL;
 29    rec.prodgroup := NULL;
 30    my_prod        := frec(rec) ;
 31    dbms_output.put_line(my_prod.prodname||' '||my_prod.prodgroup||' '||my_prod.prodprice);
 32  END;
 33
```

Collection

While record is two dimensional, a collection is a one dimension. PL/SQL has three types of collection. We will cover one type only, the associative array, which is a key-value pairs. The values are indexed; the index is the key.

To create an associate array you must first declare its type using the following syntax.

```
DECLARE TYPE associative_array_name
IS
  TABLE OF data_type INDEX BY index_data_type);
… (other declarations)
BEGIN
…
END;
```

We then use the associate array type to declare a variable of this type.

We declare an associative array aa_price in Example 10-4, and then use it to declare the prod_price variable.

An element of the array is then populated from the row of the produce table. Note the way we access the element, prod_price(v_name) using the syntax array_name(index).

The array in Example 10-4 has a **string** index; you can also have a **numeric** index.

```
Example 10-4.sql

SQL Worksheet  History

Worksheet    Query Builder

 1 ⊟ DECLARE
 2      v_name produce.name%type;
 3      v_price produce.price%type;
 4    TYPE aa_price
 5    IS
 6      TABLE OF VARCHAR2(50) INDEX BY VARCHAR2(64);
 7      prod_price aa_price;
 8    BEGIN
 9      SELECT name, price INTO v_name, v_price FROM produce WHERE code=1;
10      prod_price(v_name) := v_price;
11      dbms_output.put_line(v_name||' '||v_price);
12    END;
13
```

Similar to record, you can use array as function's parameter as well its return data type.

Methods

Built-in methods that operate on array make collections easier to use. The following table lists the available methods.

Method	Description
DELETE	Deletes elements from collection
TRIM	Deletes elements from end of collection
EXTEND	Adds elements to end of collection
EXISTS	Returns TRUE if and only if specified element exists
FIRST	Returns first index in collection
LAST	Returns last index in collection
COUNT	Returns number of elements in collection
LIMIT	Returns maximum number of elements that collection can have
PRIOR	Returns index that precedes specified index
NEXT	Returns index that succeeds specified index

Generally the syntax to invoke a method is as follows.

    array_name.method

Usage of the COUNT, FIRST, EXISTS, and DELETE methods is shown in Example 10-5.

Example 10-5.sql

SQL Worksheet | History

Worksheet | Query Builder

```sql
 1 □ DECLARE
 2     v_name produce.name%type;
 3     v_price produce.price%type;
 4    TYPE aa_price
 5    IS
 6      TABLE OF VARCHAR2(50) INDEX BY VARCHAR2(64);
 7      prod_price aa_price;
 8    BEGIN
 9      SELECT name, price INTO v_name, v_price FROM produce WHERE code=1;
10      prod_price(v_name) := v_price;
11      dbms_output.put_line(prod_price.COUNT);
12      dbms_output.put_line(prod_price.FIRST);
13 □    IF NOT prod_price.EXISTS('Carrot') THEN
14        dbms_output.put_line('Carrot not exist');
15      ELSE
16        prod_price.DELETE('Carrot');
17      END IF;
18    END;
```

Chapter 11: Granting Privileges

When you create database objects, such as table and stored program, you own the database objects. You must grant the appropriate privileges to other users who need to use the database objects. The GRANT statement has the following syntax.

```
GRANT privilege
ON object
TO user;
```

Granting on Table

To allow others to manipulate the data in a table, you need to grant one or more of SELECT, INSERT, UPDATE, and DELETE privileges. Example 11-1 grants all four privileges on the produce table to user1.

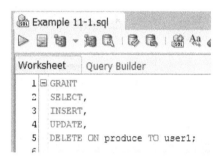

If you want to try Listing 12.1 execute the two statements in Example 11-2 to create user1 and allow it to accessing the database. Note that the user you're using to execute these statements must have the privilege to create a user.

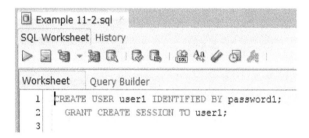

User1 can now manipulate the produce data. To confirm, you can test it by logging on (connect) as user1 and for example query the produce data.

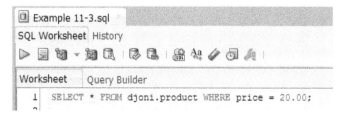

Note that user1 needs to prefix the product table with the owner (djoni) to specifically query the produce table owned by djoni.

Column Privilege

For UPDATE and INSERT privileges you can grant on selective columns. The GRANT syntax for column privilege is as follows.

```
GRANT
UPDATE|INSERT(columns) ON table TO user;
```

Example 11-4 for example grants update privilege on c_name column of the customer table.

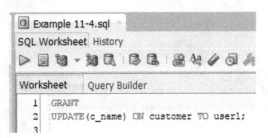

Note you cannot grant delete and select privileges on selective columns.

Granting to Public

Instead of granting privilege to a specific user, you can grant to all users using the following statement.

```
GRANT privilege
ON object
TO PUBLIC;
```

Example 11-5 grants select privilege on the produce table to all users.

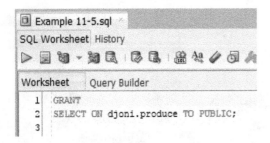

Granting to Role

A role is a set of privileges. To grant privilege by way of role, you have to go through a three steps process. First, you create a role; then, grant privileges to the role; finally grant the role to users.

Example 11-6 is an example of the process. An ins_del role is created, the role is then granted insert and delete privileges on the produce table. When the third statement is executed user1 is granted the privileges of the ins_del role.

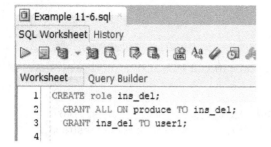

Granting on Stored Programs

To allow other users execute your programs, you grant them the EXECUTE privilege on the stored programs. Example 11-7 for example grant user1 allowing it to execute the update_price stored procedure.

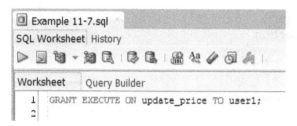

Chapter 12: PL/SLQ in Java

This chapter gives you the basic ideas of how, using JDBC, you can call PL/SQL stored procedure in a Java program.

To follow this chapter you need to have some Java skills and to try the program you must have JDBC installed on your computer. You can download Oracle JDBC from the Oracle website and follow the guide to set it up.

In general, your Java program should do the following steps:
- Import the sql, jdbc, and other required Java packages
- Create a data source object and establish a connection to the database
- Create a callable statement to call to the stored procedure and execute the statement
- Execute any other processes (none in the Example 13-1 below)
- Close the statement, and finally close the connection

In Example 12-1 the Java program executes the *execute* method of the spstmt object shown highlighted to call the update_price stored procedure (CALL update_price).

```
--Example 12-1
// Save this listing as StorProc.java file
// Import the following libraries
import java.sql.*;
import oracle.jdbc.*;
import oracle.jdbc.pool.*;
import java.math.*;
import java.io.*;
import java.awt.*;

class StorProc {
    public static void main (String args []) throws SQLException {
        // Create a data source object and connect to the database
        OracleDataSource ods = new OracleDataSource();
        ods.setURL("jdbc:oracle:thin:@//localhost:1521/xe");
        ods.setUser("djoni");
        ods.setPassword("grotto007");
        Connection conn = ods.getConnection();

        CallableStatement spstmt = conn.prepareCall ("{CALL update_price}");
        spstmt.execute();

        //Close the statement and the connection
        spstmt.close();
        conn.close();
    }
}
```

Create the update_price stored procedure by executing the following statement.

```
-- Example 12-2
CREATE PROCEDURE update_price
AS
  avgprc NUMBER(6,2);
BEGIN
```

```
 SELECT AVG(price) INTO avgprc FROM produce;
 UPDATE produce SET price = price + (price * 0.10) WHERE price < avgprc;
END update_price;
```

Compile the StorProc.java source program and then execute it.

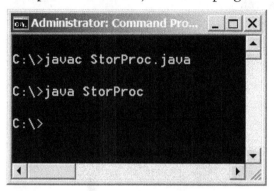

When you check the produce table, prices lower than the average would have been updated as specified in the stored procedure.

Appendix A: Source Codes

When you try an example, but don't want to type the source code, you can copy it from the listing in this appendix and paste it on your SQL Developer worksheet.

```sql
-- create_produce.sql
CREATE TABLE produce
(code INTEGER PRIMARY KEY,
name VARCHAR2(20),
type CHAR(6),
price NUMBER(4,2),
update_dt DATE);
```

```sql
-- insert_produce.sql
INSERT INTO produce VALUES(1, 'Apple','Fruit',1,to_date('1-MAY-2014','DD-MON-YYYY'));
INSERT INTO produce VALUES(2,'Broccoli','Veggie',2,to_date('2-MAY-2014','DD-MON-YYYY'));
INSERT INTO produce VALUES(3 ,'Carrot','Veggie',3,to_date('3-MAY-2014','DD-MON-YYYY'));
INSERT INTO produce VALUES(4,'Mango','Fruit',4,to_date('4-MAY-2014','DD-MON-YYYY'));
INSERT INTO produce VALUES(5,'Grape','Fruit',5,to_date('5-MAY-2014','DD-MON-YYYY'));
```

```sql
-- running_plsql.sql
DECLARE
  code_var          INTEGER;
  type_var          CHAR(6);
  name_var          VARCHAR2 (20);
  price_var         NUMBER(4,2);
  update_dt_var     DATE;
  price_too_high EXCEPTION;
BEGIN
  SELECT code,type,name,price,update_dt
  INTO code_var,type_var,name_var,price_var,update_dt_var
  FROM produce
  WHERE name   = 'Grape';
  IF price_var > 4.5 THEN
    RAISE price_too_high;
  END IF;
EXCEPTION
WHEN price_too_high THEN
  dbms_output.put_line ('Price is too high');
END;
```

```sql
-- create_prodlog.sql

CREATE TABLE prodlog (log_date DATE, p_code VARCHAR2(6));
```

```sql
-- Example 3-1
DECLARE
  code_var          INTEGER;
  type_var          CHAR(6);
  name_var          VARCHAR2 (20);
  price_var         NUMBER(4,2);
  update_dt_var DATE;
```

```
BEGIN
  SELECT code, type, name, price, update_dt
  INTO code_var, type_var, name_var, price_var, update_dt_var
  FROM produce
  WHERE name = 'Apple';
  dbms_output.put_line(code_var||' '||type_var||' '||name_var
  ||' '||price_var||' '||update_dt_var);
END;
```

-- Example 3-2
```
DECLARE
  type_var        CHAR(6);
  name_var        VARCHAR2 (20);
  price_var       NUMBER(4,2);
  update_dt_var DATE;
BEGIN
  SELECT code, type, name, price, update_dt
  INTO code_var, type_var, name_var, price_var, update_dt_var
  FROM produce
  WHERE name = 'Apple';
END;
```

-- Example 3-3
```
BEGIN
  dbms_output.put_line('Welcome to PL/SQL!');
END;
```

-- Example 3-4
```
DECLARE
  x VARCHAR2(5);
BEGIN
  x := 'abcdef';
  dbms_output.put_line('Error');
END;
```

-- Example 3-5
```
DECLARE
  x VARCHAR2(5);
BEGIN
  x := 'abcdef';
EXCEPTION
WHEN OTHERS THEN
  dbms_output.put_line('Error');
END;
```

-- Example 3-6
```
BEGIN
  dbms_output.put_line('Parent block');
  BEGIN
    dbms_output.put_line('  First child nested block');
  END;
  BEGIN
      dbms_output.put_line('  Second child nested block');
   BEGIN
    dbms_output.put_line('    Grandchild nested block of 1st child');
   END;
  END;
```

```
END;

-- Example 3-7
<< parent >>
BEGIN
  dbms_output.put_line('Parent block');
  << first_child >>
  BEGIN
    dbms_output.put_line('  First child nested block');
  END first_child;
  << second_child >>
  BEGIN
      dbms_output.put_line('  Second child nested block');
    << grandchild >>
     BEGIN
      dbms_output.put_line('    Grandchild nested block of 1st child');
     END grandchild;
  END second_child;
END parent;

-- Example 3-8
DECLARE
  code_var      INTEGER;
  type_var      CHAR(6);
  name_var      VARCHAR2 (20);
  price_var     NUMBER(4,2);
  update_dt_var DATE;
BEGIN
  SELECT code, type, name, price, update_dt
  INTO code_var, type_var, name_var, price_var, update_dt_var
  FROM produce
  WHERE name = 'Pineapple';
  dbms_output.put_line (code_var||' '||type_var||' '||
  name_var ||' '||price_var ||' '||update_dt_var);
EXCEPTION
WHEN OTHERS THEN
  << parent_block >>
  BEGIN
    IF SQLCODE IN(+100, -1422) THEN
      <<child_block>>
      BEGIN
        IF SQLCODE = +100 THEN
          dbms_output.put_line('there is no Pineapple');
        ELSE
          dbms_output.put_line('query returns more than one row');
        END IF;
      END child_block;
    END IF;
  END parent_block;
END;

-- Example 3-9
<< parent >>
DECLARE
parent_var VARCHAR2(10) := 'parent';
BEGIN
  dbms_output.put_line(parent_var);
```

```
  << first_child >>
  DECLARE
  first_child_var VARCHAR2(10) := 'child';
  BEGIN
    dbms_output.put_line(first_child_var);
    dbms_output.put_line(parent_var);
  END first_child;
END parent;
```

-- Example 3-10
```
<< parent >>
DECLARE
  parent_var VARCHAR2(10) := 'parent';
BEGIN
  dbms_output.put_line(parent_var);
  dbms_output.put_line(first_child_var);
  << first_child >>
  DECLARE
    first_child_var VARCHAR2(10) := 'child';
  BEGIN
    dbms_output.put_line(first_child_var);
    dbms_output.put_line(parent_var);
  END first_child;
  << second_child >>
  BEGIN
    dbms_output.put_line(first_child_var);
  END second_child;
END parent;
```

-- Example 3-11
```
<< parent >>
DECLARE
  same_name_var VARCHAR2(10) := 'parent';
BEGIN
  dbms_output.put_line(same_name_var);
  << child >>
  DECLARE
    same_name_var VARCHAR2(10) := 'child';
  BEGIN
    dbms_output.put_line(same_name_var);
    dbms_output.put_line(parent.same_name_var);
  END child;
END parent;
```

-- Example 3-12
```
-- Example 3-12: Comments
-- An example of declaring a constant and a variable
DECLARE
  fruit_con  CONSTANT VARCHAR2(20) := 'Fruit';  -- constant example
  veggie_var VARCHAR2(20)          := 'Veggie'; -- variable example
BEGIN
  /* the following SQL adds a produce
  into the produce table */
  INSERT
  INTO produce VALUES
    (99,'Tangerine',fruit_con, 9 , '1-JAN-2014' );
END;
```

```
-- Example 4-1
DECLARE
  code_var        INTEGER;
  type_var        CHAR(6);
  name_var        VARCHAR2 (20);
  price_var       NUMBER(4,2);
  update_dt_var DATE;
BEGIN
  SELECT code, type, name, price, update_dt
  INTO code_var, type_var, name_var, price_var, update_dt_var
  FROM produce
  WHERE name = 'Apple';
  dbms_output.put_line (code_var||' '||type_var||' '||name_var
  ||' '||price_var||' '||update_dt_var);
END;

-- Example 4-2
DECLARE
  code_var        INTEGER;
  name_var        VARCHAR2 (20);
  price_var       NUMBER(4,2);
  update_dt_var DATE;
  new_name_var VARCHAR2(20);
BEGIN
  SELECT code, name, price, update_dt
  INTO code_var, name_var, price_var, update_dt_var
  FROM produce
  WHERE name = 'Apple';
  new_name_var   := 'New ' || name_var;
  dbms_output.put_line
  (code_var||' '||new_name_var||' '||price_var||' '||update_dt_var);
  UPDATE produce SET name = new_name_var WHERE code = code_var;
END;

-- Example 4-3
DECLARE
  code_var        INTEGER;
  type_var        CHAR(10);
  name_var        VARCHAR2(20);
  price_var       NUMBER(4,2);
  update_dt_var DATE;
  new_name_var  VARCHAR2(20);
  new_var   VARCHAR2 (20) DEFAULT 'New ';
BEGIN
  SELECT code, type, name, price, update_dt
  INTO code_var, type_var, name_var, price_var, update_dt_var
  FROM produce
  WHERE name    = 'Grape';
  new_name_var := new_var || name_var;
  dbms_output.put_line (code_var||' '||new_name_var||' '||price_var||' '||
  update_dt_var);
  UPDATE produce SET name = new_name_var WHERE code = code_var;
END;

-- Example 4-4
DECLARE
```

```
  code_var        INTEGER;
  type_var        CHAR(10) := 'Fruit';
  name_var        VARCHAR2(20);
  price_var       NUMBER(4,2);
  update_dt_var   DATE;
  new_name_var    VARCHAR(20);
  new_var         CHAR (4) DEFAULT 'New ';
BEGIN
  dbms_output.put_line('The value of type_var is: ' || type_var);
  SELECT *
  INTO code_var,type_var,name_var,price_var,update_dt_var
  FROM produce
  WHERE code = 99;
  dbms_output.put_line('The value of type_var is: ' || type_var);
END;
```

-- Example 4-5
```
DECLARE
  code_var        INTEGER;
  type_var        CHAR(10) NOT NULL := 'Fruit';
  name_var        VARCHAR2(20);
  price_var       NUMBER(6,2);
  update_dt_var   DATE;
  new_name_var    VARCHAR(20);
  new_var         CHAR (4) DEFAULT 'New ';
BEGIN
  SELECT code, type, name, price, update_dt
  INTO code_var, type_var, name_var, price_var, update_dt_var
  FROM produce
  WHERE code = 99;
  dbms_output.put_line('The value of type_var is: ' || type_var);
END;
```

-- Example 4-6
```
DECLARE
  fruit_con   CONSTANT VARCHAR2(20) := 'Fruit';
  veggie_con  CONSTANT VARCHAR2(20) := 'Veggie';
BEGIN
  INSERT INTO produce VALUES
    (11, 'Tangerine', fruit_con ,11,'11-MAY-2014');
  INSERT INTO produce VALUES
    (12, 'Lettuce', veggie_con ,12,'12-MAY-2014');
END;
```

-- Example 4-7
```
DECLARE
  fruit_con   CONSTANT VARCHAR2(20) := 'Fruit';
  veggie_con  CONSTANT VARCHAR2(20) := 'Veggie';
BEGIN
  fruit_con := 'New Fruit';
END;
```

-- Example 5-1
```
DECLARE
  code_var        INTEGER;
  type_var        CHAR(10) NOT NULL := 'Veggie';
  name_var        VARCHAR2(20);
```

```
  price_var      NUMBER(6,2) := 2.5;
  update_dt_var DATE;
BEGIN
  code_var  := 20;
  name_var  := 'Kale';
  price_var := price_var + 1.0;
  update_dt_var := CURRENT_DATE;
  INSERT INTO produce VALUES
    (code_var, type_var, name_var, price_var, update_dt_var) ;
END;
```

-- Example 5-2
```
DECLARE
  num NUMBER(6,2) := &num_input;
  greater_than_10 BOOLEAN      := num > 10;
BEGIN
  IF greater_than_10 THEN
    dbms_output.put_line(num || ' is greater than 10');
    num := ROUND(num);
    dbms_output.put_line(num || ' rounded' );
  END IF;
END;
```

-- Example 5-3
```
DECLARE
  num NUMBER(6,2) := &num_input;
  greater_than_10 BOOLEAN      := num > 10;
BEGIN
  IF greater_than_10 THEN
    dbms_output.put_line(num || ' is greater than 10');
    num := ROUND(num);
    dbms_output.put_line(num || ' rounded' );
  END IF;
END;
```

-- Example 5-4
```
DECLARE
  num              NUMBER(6,2) := &num_input;
  greater_than_10 BOOLEAN      := num > 10;
BEGIN
  IF greater_than_10 THEN
    dbms_output.put_line(num || ' is greater than 10');
  ELSE
    dbms_output.put_line(num || ' is equal or smaller than 10');
  END IF;
END;
```

-- Example 5-5
```
DECLARE
  num              NUMBER(6,2) := &num_input;
  greater_than_10 BOOLEAN      := num > 10;
BEGIN
  IF greater_than_10 THEN
    dbms_output.put_line(num || ' is greater than 10');
  ELSIF num = 10 THEN
    dbms_output.put_line(num || ' is equal to 10');
  ELSE
```

```
    dbms_output.put_line(num || ' is smaller than 10');
  END IF;
END;


-- Example 5-6
DECLARE
  clue VARCHAR2(1) := '&clue_input';
BEGIN
  CASE clue
  WHEN 'O' THEN
    DBMS_OUTPUT.PUT_LINE('Obvious');
  WHEN 'U' THEN
    DBMS_OUTPUT.PUT_LINE('Useless');
  WHEN 'N' THEN
    DBMS_OUTPUT.PUT_LINE('Not Sure');
  WHEN 'M' THEN
    DBMS_OUTPUT.PUT_LINE('Need More');
  ELSE
    DBMS_OUTPUT.PUT_LINE('Input Not Valid');
  END CASE;
END;


-- Example 5-7
DECLARE
  sel         NUMBER(1)   := &sel_in;
  sel_value_1 VARCHAR2(2) := '&sel_in_1';
  sel_value_2 VARCHAR2(2) := '&sel_in_2';
BEGIN
  CASE (sel)
  WHEN sel_value_1 THEN
    DBMS_OUTPUT.PUT_LINE('sel = sel_value_1');
  WHEN sel_value_2 THEN
    DBMS_OUTPUT.PUT_LINE('sel = sel_value_2');
  ELSE
    DBMS_OUTPUT.PUT_LINE('Input Not Valid ');
  END CASE;
END;


-- Example 5-8
DECLARE
  max_price DECIMAL(6,2);
  avg_price DECIMAL(6,2);
BEGIN
  SELECT MAX(price) INTO max_price FROM produce;
  SELECT AVG(price) INTO avg_price FROM produce;
  CASE
    -- reduce price
  WHEN max_price > 5 THEN
    UPDATE produce SET price = price - (price * .01);
    -- increase price
  WHEN avg_price < 3.5 THEN
    UPDATE produce SET price = price + (price * .01);
  END CASE;
END;


-- Example 5-9
DECLARE
```

```
   num NUMBER := 1;
BEGIN
  << basic_loop >>
  LOOP
    IF num > 3 THEN -- loop three times only
      EXIT;
    END IF;
    DBMS_OUTPUT.PUT_LINE ('In loop: num = ' || TO_CHAR(num));
    num := num + 1;
  END LOOP basic_loop;
  -- On EXIT, execute the following statement
  DBMS_OUTPUT.PUT_LINE('After loop: num = ' || TO_CHAR(num));
END;


-- Example 5-10
DECLARE
  counter1 NUMBER := 1;
  counter2 NUMBER := 1;
BEGIN
  LOOP
    IF counter1 > 2 THEN EXIT; -- loop twice
    END IF;
    DBMS_OUTPUT.PUT_LINE ('Outer loop: counter1 = ' || TO_CHAR(counter1));
    counter1 := counter1 + 1;
    LOOP
      IF counter2 > 2 THEN EXIT; -- loop twice
      END IF;
      DBMS_OUTPUT.PUT_LINE ('Inner loop: counter2 = ' || TO_CHAR(counter2));
      counter2 := counter2 + 1;
    END LOOP;
    counter2 := 1;
  END LOOP;
  DBMS_OUTPUT.PUT_LINE('After loop: counter1 = ' || TO_CHAR(counter1));
END;


-- Example 5-11
BEGIN
  FOR i IN 1..3
  LOOP
    dbms_output.put_line('Iteration number: '||i);
  END LOOP;
END;


-- Example 5-12
DECLARE
  i INTEGER := 1;
BEGIN
  WHILE i < 4
  LOOP
    dbms_output.put_line('Iteration number: '||i);
    i := i +1;
  END LOOP;
END;


-- Example 6-1
DECLARE
  code_var        INTEGER;
```

```
  type_var        CHAR(6);
  name_var        VARCHAR2 (20);
  price_var       NUMBER(6,2);
  update_dt_var DATE;
BEGIN
  SELECT code, type, name, price, update_dt
  INTO code_var, type_var, name_var, price_var, update_dt_var
  FROM produce
  WHERE name = 'Pineapple';
  dbms_output.put_line (code_var||' '||type_var||' '||name_var
  ||' '||price_var||' '||update_dt_var);
END;
```

-- Example 6-2

```
DECLARE
  code_var        INTEGER;
  type_var        CHAR(6);
  name_var        VARCHAR2 (20);
  price_var       NUMBER(6,2);
  update_dt_var DATE;
BEGIN
  SELECT code, type, name, price, update_dt
  INTO code_var, type_var, name_var, price_var, update_dt_var
  FROM produce
  WHERE name = 'Pineapple';
  dbms_output.put_line (code_var||' '||type_var||' '||name_var
  ||' '||price_var||' '||update_dt_var);
EXCEPTION
WHEN no_data_found THEN
  dbms_output.put_line('Our query does not find any Pineapple.');
END;
```

-- Example 6-3

```
<< parent >>
DECLARE
  code_v VARCHAR2(20);
BEGIN
  dbms_output.put_line ('Parent');
  << first_child >>
  BEGIN
    SELECT code INTO code_v FROM produce WHERE name = 'Pineapple';
  EXCEPTION
  WHEN TOO_MANY_ROWS THEN
    dbms_output.put_line ('First_child Exception');
  END first_child;
  EXCEPTION
WHEN OTHERS THEN
  dbms_output.put_line ('Parent Exception');
END parent;
```

-- Example 6-4

```
DECLARE
  code_v VARCHAR2(20);
BEGIN
  SELECT code INTO code_v FROM produce WHERE name = 'Pineapple';
EXCEPTION
WHEN TOO_MANY_ROWS OR no_data_found THEN
```

```
    dbms_output.put_line ('Error with the Query');
END;


-- Example 6-5
<< parent >>
DECLARE
    code_v VARCHAR2(20);
BEGIN
    dbms_output.put_line ('Parent');
    SELECT code INTO code_v FROM produce WHERE name = 'Guava';
    << first_child >>
    BEGIN
        SELECT code INTO code_v FROM produce WHERE name = 'Apple';
    EXCEPTION
    WHEN no_data_found THEN
        dbms_output.put_line ('First_child Exception');
    END first_child;
    EXCEPTION
WHEN TOO_MANY_ROWS THEN
    dbms_output.put_line ('Parent Exception');
END parent;


-- Example 6-6
<< parent >>
DECLARE
    code_v VARCHAR2(20);
BEGIN
    dbms_output.put_line ('Parent');
    << first_child >>
    BEGIN
        SELECT code INTO code_v FROM produce WHERE name = 'Pineapple';
    EXCEPTION
    WHEN TOO_MANY_ROWS THEN
        dbms_output.put_line ('First_child Exception');
    END first_child;
    EXCEPTION
WHEN no_data_found THEN
    dbms_output.put_line ('Parent Exception');
END parent;


-- Example 6-7
DECLARE
    x VARCHAR2(5);
BEGIN
    x := 'abcdef';
    dbms_output.put_line('Error');
EXCEPTION
WHEN VALUE_ERROR THEN
    dbms_output.put_line
    ('We have an error related to data value');
END;


-- Example 6-8
DECLARE
    x VARCHAR2(5);
BEGIN
    x := 'abcdef';
```

```
EXCEPTION
WHEN VALUE_ERROR THEN
  dbms_output.put_line('The error code is: ' ||SQLCODE);
  dbms_output.put_line('The error message is: '||SQLERRM);
END;


-- Example 6-9
DECLARE
  pk_violation EXCEPTION;
  PRAGMA EXCEPTION_INIT(pk_violation, -1);
BEGIN
  UPDATE produce SET code = 1 WHERE code = 2;
EXCEPTION
WHEN pk_violation THEN
  dbms_output.put_line (SQLCODE);
  dbms_output.put_line (SQLERRM);
END;


-- Example 7-1
DECLARE
  avg_price NUMBER(6,2);
BEGIN
  SELECT AVG(price)
  INTO avg_price
  FROM produce;
  dbms_output.put_line('The average price is: ' || avg_price);
  UPDATE produce
  SET price   = price + 0.10 * avg_price
  WHERE price < avg_price;
END;


-- Example 7-2
DECLARE
  code_v  VARCHAR2(20);
  name_v  VARCHAR2(20);
  price_v NUMBER(6,2);
BEGIN
  SELECT code, name, price
  INTO code_v, name_v, price_v
  FROM produce
  WHERE name = 'Apple';
  dbms_output.put_line(
  'The price of our ' ||name_v||
  ' (its code is '||(code_v)|| ') is $'
  || price_v);
END;


-- Example 7-3
DECLARE
  code_v  VARCHAR2(20);
  name_v  VARCHAR2(20);
  price_v NUMBER(6,2);
BEGIN
  SELECT code, name, price
  INTO code_v, name_v, price_v
  FROM produce;
  dbms_output.put_line(
```

```
  'The price of our ' ||name_v||
  ' (its code is '||(code_v)|| ') is $'
  || price_v);
END;
```

-- Example 7-4

```
DECLARE
  code_v  VARCHAR2(20);
  name_v  VARCHAR2(20);
  price_v NUMBER(6,2);
BEGIN
  SELECT code, name, price
  INTO code_v, name_v, price_v
  FROM produce
  WHERE type = 'Veggie';
EXCEPTION
WHEN too_many_rows THEN
dbms_output.put_line('Error: More than one row returned');
END;
```

-- Example 7-5

```
DECLARE
  avg_price produce.price%TYPE;
  p_row produce%ROWTYPE;
BEGIN
  SELECT *
  INTO p_row
  FROM produce
  WHERE name = 'Carrot';
  dbms_output.put_line('The price of our '||p_row.name
  ||' (its code is '||p_row.code|| ') is $'||p_row.price);
END;
```

-- Example 7-6

```
DECLARE
  p_row produce%ROWTYPE;
  price_count INTEGER := 0;
BEGIN
  SELECT * INTO p_row FROM produce
  WHERE name = 'Apple' FOR UPDATE OF price;
  UPDATE produce SET price  = 1 WHERE name = 'Apple';
END;
```

-- Example 7-7

```
DECLARE
  p_row produce%ROWTYPE;
  price_count INTEGER := 0;
BEGIN
  SELECT * INTO p_row FROM produce
  WHERE name = 'Apple' FOR UPDATE OF price;
  UPDATE produce SET price  = 1.5 WHERE name = 'Apple';
  SELECT COUNT(*) INTO price_count FROM produce
  WHERE price    = 1.5;
  IF price_count > 1 THEN
    ROLLBACK;
  ELSE
    COMMIT;
```

```
     END IF;
END;
```

--Example 7-8

```
DECLARE
  avgprc NUMBER(6,2);
BEGIN
  SELECT AVG(price) INTO avgprc FROM product;
  UPDATE product SET price = price + (price * 0.10) WHERE price < avgprc;
  UPDATE product SET price = price + (price * 0.01) WHERE price > avgprc;
  SELECT AVG(price) INTO avgprc FROM product;
   IF avgprc > 10.00 THEN ROLLBACK;
   END IF;
  COMMIT;
END;
```

--Example 7-9

```
DECLARE
  avgprc NUMBER(6,2);
BEGIN
  SELECT AVG(price) INTO avgprc FROM produce;
  UPDATE produce SET price = price + (price * 0.10) WHERE price < avgprc;
  INSERT
  INTO produce VALUES
    (
      999,'Kale',
      'V', 1.50,
      to_date('1-5-2013','DD-MM-YYYY')
    );
  SAVEPOINT after_insert;
  UPDATE produce SET price = price + (price * 0.01) WHERE price > avgprc;
  SELECT AVG(price) INTO avgprc FROM produce;
  IF avgprc > 2.00 THEN
    ROLLBACK TO after_insert;
  END IF;
  COMMIT;
END;
```

--Example 7-10

```
DECLARE
  avgprc NUMBER(6,2);
BEGIN
  SET TRANSACTION NAME 't1';
  INSERT
  INTO produce VALUES
    (
      99,'Mellon',
      'F', 5.50,
      to_date('1-5-2013','DD-MM-YYYY')
    );
  COMMIT;
  SET TRANSACTION NAME 't2';
  UPDATE produce SET price = price + (price * 0.10) WHERE price > avgprc;
  SELECT AVG(price) INTO avgprc FROM produce;
  IF avgprc > 12.00 THEN
    ROLLBACK;
```

```
    END IF;
    COMMIT;
END;


-- Example 7-11
BEGIN
  EXECUTE immediate 'CREATE TABLE sample_produce (code INTEGER, name
varchar2(20), price NUMBER(4,2))';
END;


-- Example 8-1
DECLARE CURSOR c_produce IS SELECT * FROM produce;
v_produce c_produce% rowtype;
BEGIN
OPEN c_produce;
FETCH c_produce INTO v_produce;
dbms_output.put_line( v_produce.code || ' '||v_produce.name);
CLOSE c_produce;
END;


-- Example 8-1.1
DECLARE
  CURSOR c_produce (c_lowprice NUMBER, c_highprice NUMBER)
  IS
    SELECT * FROM produce WHERE price BETWEEN c_lowprice AND c_highprice;
  v_produce c_produce%rowtype;
BEGIN
  OPEN c_produce (2, 4);
  FETCH c_produce INTO v_produce;
  dbms_output.put_line( v_produce.code ||' '||v_produce.name ||' '||
v_produce.price);
  CLOSE c_produce;
END;




-- Example 8-2
DECLARE
  price_increase NUMBER(2,2) := 0.01;
  CURSOR c
  IS
    SELECT price, (price + price_increase) new_price
    FROM produce;
  cr c%rowtype;
BEGIN
  OPEN c;
  FETCH c INTO cr;
  dbms_output.put_line('The current price of ' || cr.price ||
  ' will increase to ' || cr.new_price);
END;


-- Example 8-3
DECLARE
  CURSOR c
  IS
    SELECT * FROM produce;
  cr c%rowtype;
```

```
    i INTEGER := 1;
BEGIN
  OPEN c;
  WHILE i < 7
  LOOP
    FETCH c INTO cr;
    dbms_output.put_line(cr.code);
    i := i + 1;
  END LOOP;
  CLOSE c;
END;
```

-- **Example 8-4**
```
DECLARE
  CURSOR c
  IS
    SELECT * FROM produce;
  cr c%rowtype;
BEGIN
  OPEN c;
  LOOP
    FETCH c INTO cr;
    EXIT
  WHEN c%notfound;
    dbms_output.put_line(cr.code || ' - ' || cr.name);
  END LOOP;
  CLOSE c;
END;
```

-- **Example 8-5**
```
DECLARE
  CURSOR c
  IS SELECT name FROM produce;
  name_c VARCHAR2(5);
  s       VARCHAR2(15);
BEGIN
  OPEN c;
  LOOP FETCH c INTO name_c;
    EXIT WHEN c%notfound;
  END LOOP;
  EXCEPTION
WHEN OTHERS THEN
  IF c%ISOPEN THEN s := 'c is still Open';
    dbms_output.put_line(s);
    dbms_output.put_line(SQLERRM);
    CLOSE c;
  END IF;
END;
```

-- **Example 8-6**
```
DECLARE
  CURSOR c
  IS
    SELECT code, name
    FROM produce
    WHERE type = 'Veggie';
BEGIN
```

```
    FOR c_index IN c
    LOOP
      dbms_output.put_line(c_index.code ||' '|| c_index.name);
    END LOOP;
END;


-- Example 8-7
DECLARE
  output VARCHAR2(40);
BEGIN
  FOR p_row IN
  (SELECT * FROM produce)
  LOOP
    Output := 'The name of this ' || p_row.type || ' is: ' || p_row.name;
    dbms_output.put_line(output);
  END LOOP;
END;


-- Example 8-8
DECLARE
  cr produce_v%rowtype;
BEGIN
  FOR c IN
  (
    SELECT * FROM produce_v order by code
  )
  LOOP
    cr := c;
    dbms_output.put_line
    (cr.code ||' '|| cr.name||' '||cr.price);
  END LOOP;
END;


-- Example 9-1
DECLARE
  name_uc produce.name%type;
  FUNCTION uc_name(
      code_p produce.code%type)
   RETURN VARCHAR2
  IS
    name_v produce.name%type; -- variable declaration within the function's
Declaration part
  BEGIN
    SELECT upper(name)
    INTO name_v
    FROM produce
    WHERE code = code_p; -- Executable part
    RETURN name_v;
  EXCEPTION -- Exception part
  WHEN OTHERS THEN
    RETURN 'Error'; -- the function returns an Error when the produce code is
not in the produce table
  END uc_name;
  BEGIN -- the start of the program's Executable part
    FOR p IN
    (SELECT * FROM produce /*--WHERE code < 9*/
    )
```

```
      LOOP
         name_uc := uc_name(p.code); -- use the function
         dbms_output.put_line(p.code||' '||name_uc);
      END LOOP;
      dbms_output.put_line(uc_name(9)); -- use the function again; here the
function returns an Error
   END;
```

-- Example 9-2
```
DECLARE
PROCEDURE update_price(
      name_p produce.name%type)
IS
   p_row produce%rowtype;
BEGIN
   SELECT * INTO p_row FROM produce
   WHERE name = name_p FOR UPDATE OF price;
   UPDATE produce SET price = price+(price*0.1)
   WHERE name = name_p;
END update_price; -- enf of procedure
BEGIN                -- now use the procedure
   update_price('Apple');
   update_price('Carrot');
END;
```

-- Example 9-3
```
CREATE FUNCTION uc_name(
      cp_code produce.code%type)
   RETURN VARCHAR2
IS
   name_v VARCHAR2(50);
BEGIN
   SELECT upper(name) INTO name_v FROM produce WHERE code = cp_code;
   RETURN name_v;
EXCEPTION
WHEN OTHERS THEN
   RETURN 'Error';
END uc_name;
```

-- Example 9-4
```
CREATE PROCEDURE update_price(
      cp_name produce.name%type)
AS
   v_produce produce%rowtype;
BEGIN
   SELECT * INTO v_produce FROM produce WHERE name = cp_name FOR UPDATE OF
price;
   UPDATE produce SET price = price+(price*0.1) WHERE name = cp_name;
END update_price;
```

-- Example 9-5
```
DECLARE
   v_name produce.name%type;
BEGIN
   FOR p IN
```

```
   (SELECT * FROM produce
   )
   LOOP
     v_name:=un_name(p.code);
     dbms_output.put_line(p.code||' '||v_name);
   END LOOP;
END;
```

-- Example 9-6
```
BEGIN
  update_price('Apple');
  update_price('Carrot');
END;
```

-- Example 9-7
```
CREATE PACKAGE mypackage
AS
   FUNCTION uc_name(
       cp_code produce.code%type)
     RETURN VARCHAR2;
   PROCEDURE update_price(
       cp_name produce.name%type);
END mypackage;
```

-- Example 9-8
```
CREATE OR REPLACE PACKAGE body mypackage
AS
   FUNCTION uc_name(
       cp_code produce.code%type)
     RETURN VARCHAR2
   IS
     name_v VARCHAR2(50);
   BEGIN
     SELECT upper(name) INTO name_v FROM produce WHERE code = cp_code;
     RETURN name_v;
   EXCEPTION
   WHEN OTHERS THEN
     RETURN 'Error';
   END uc_name;
   PROCEDURE update_price(
       cp_name produce.name%type)
   AS
     v_produce produce%rowtype;
   BEGIN
     SELECT * INTO v_produce FROM produce WHERE name = cp_name FOR UPDATE OF
price;
     UPDATE produce SET price = price+(price*0.1) WHERE name = cp_name;
   END update_price;
END mypackage;
```

--Example 9-9
```
CREATE TRIGGER t_prodlog
  BEFORE DELETE OR INSERT ON produce
BEGIN
```

```
  INSERT INTO prodlog (log_date)
    VALUES (SYSDATE);
END;
```

-- Example 9-10

```
CREATE TRIGGER tc_prodlog_when AFTER
  UPDATE ON produce FOR EACH ROW WHEN (NEW.price > 2.00)
BEGIN
  INSERT INTO prodlog
    (log_date) VALUES (SYSDATE);
END;
```

-- Example 9-11

```
CREATE TRIGGER tcc_prodlog_when AFTER
  UPDATE OF price ON produce FOR EACH ROW WHEN (NEW.price > 2.00)
BEGIN
  INSERT INTO prodlog (log_date )
  VALUES (SYSDATE);
END;
```

-- Example 9-12

```
CREATE TRIGGER t_storproc AFTER
  DELETE ON produce
BEGIN update_price('Carrot');
END;
```

-- Example 10-1

```
DECLARE
  CURSOR c_produce (c_lowprice NUMBER, c_highprice NUMBER)
  IS
    SELECT * FROM produce WHERE price BETWEEN c_lowprice AND c_highprice;
  v_produce c_produce%rowtype;
BEGIN
  OPEN c_produce (2, 4);
  FETCH c_produce INTO v_produce;
  dbms_output.put_line( v_produce.code ||' '||v_produce.name ||' '||
v_produce.price);
  CLOSE c_produce;
END;
```

-- Example 10-2

```
DECLARE
TYPE prodtyp
IS
  RECORD
  (
    prodname  VARCHAR2(30) NOT NULL := 'initial value',
    prodprice NUMBER,
    prodgroup produce.p_group%TYPE);
  prod_rec prodtyp;
  my_prod prodtyp;
BEGIN
```

```
  SELECT name, price, p_group INTO prod_rec FROM produce WHERE code=1;
  my_prod := prod_rec;
  dbms_output.put_line(my_prod.prodname||' '||my_prod.prodprice);
END;


-- Example 10-3
DECLARE
TYPE prodtyp
IS
  RECORD
  (
    prodname  VARCHAR2(30) NOT NULL := 'initial value',
    prodprice NUMBER,
    prodgroup produce.p_group%TYPE);
  prod_rec prodtyp;
  my_prod prodtyp;
  rec prodtyp;
FUNCTION frec(
    fp_prod_rec prodtyp)
  RETURN prodtyp
IS
BEGIN
  SELECT name,
    price,
    p_group
  INTO prod_rec
  FROM produce
  WHERE name = fp_prod_rec.prodname;
  my_prod    := prod_rec;
  RETURN my_prod;
END frec;
BEGIN
  rec.prodname  := 'Carrot';
  rec.prodprice := NULL;
  rec.prodgroup := NULL;
  my_prod       := frec(rec) ;
  dbms_output.put_line(my_prod.prodname||' '||my_prod.prodgroup||'
'||my_prod.prodprice);
END;


-- Example 10-4
DECLARE
v_name produce.name%type;
v_price produce.price%type;
TYPE aa_price
IS
  TABLE OF VARCHAR2(50) INDEX BY VARCHAR2(64);
prod_price aa_price;
BEGIN
select name, price into v_name, v_price from produce where code=1;
prod_price(v_name) := v_price;
dbms_output.put_line(v_name||' '||v_price);
END;


-- Example 10-5
```

```
DECLARE
  v_name produce.name%type;
  v_price produce.price%type;
TYPE aa_price
IS
  TABLE OF VARCHAR2(50) INDEX BY VARCHAR2(64);
  prod_price aa_price;
BEGIN
  SELECT name, price INTO v_name, v_price FROM produce WHERE code=1;
  prod_price(v_name) := v_price;
    dbms_output.put_line(prod_price.COUNT);
    dbms_output.put_line(prod_price.FIRST);
  IF NOT prod_price.EXISTS('Carrot') THEN
    dbms_output.put_line('Carrot not exist');
  ELSE
    prod_price.DELETE('Carrot');
  END IF;
END;
```

-- Example 11-1

```
GRANT SELECT, INSERT, UPDATE, DELETE ON produce
TO user1;
```

-- Example 11-2

```
CREATE USER user1
IDENTIFIED by password1;
GRANT CREATE SESSION to user1;
```

-- Example 11-3

```
SELECT * FROM djoni.product WHERE price = 20.00;
```

-- Example 11-4

```
GRANT
UPDATE(c_name) ON customer TO user1;
```

-- Example 11-5

```
GRANT SELECT ON djoni.produce TO PUBLIC;
```

-- Example 11-6

```
CREATE role ins_del;
GRANT ALL ON produce TO ins_del;
GRANT ins_del TO user1;
```

-- Example 11-7

```
GRANT EXECUTE ON update_price TO user1;
```

--Example 12-1

```java
// Save this listing as StorProc.java file
// Import the following libraries
import java.sql.*;
import oracle.jdbc.*;
import oracle.jdbc.pool.*;
import java.math.*;
import java.io.*;
import java.awt.*;

class StorProc {
    public static void main (String args []) throws SQLException {
        // Create a data source object and connect to the database
        OracleDataSource ods = new OracleDataSource();
        ods.setURL("jdbc:oracle:thin:@//localhost:1521/xe");
        ods.setUser("djoni");
        ods.setPassword("grotto007");
        Connection conn = ods.getConnection();

        CallableStatement spstmt = conn.prepareCall ("{CALL update_price}");
        spstmt.execute();

        //Close the statement and the connection
        spstmt.close();
        conn.close();
    }
}
```

-- Example 12-2

```sql
CREATE PROCEDURE update_price
AS
  avgprc NUMBER(6,2);
BEGIN
  SELECT AVG(price) INTO avgprc FROM produce;
  UPDATE produce SET price = price + (price * 0.10) WHERE price < avgprc;
END update_price;
```

Index